Published by Forefront Books

Cover Design by Bruce Gore, Gore Studio Inc.
Interior Design by Bill Kersey, KerseyGraphics

ISBN: 978-1-948-67775-2
ISBN: 978-1-948-67776-9 (eBook)

Printed in the United States of America
21 23 23 24 25 5 4 3 2 1

SURVIVE

ALIVE

THRIVE

SURVIVE
— ALIVE —
THRIVE

*Navigating
the Journey from
Loss to Hope to
Happiness*

MARK S. NEGLEY

Forefront
BOOKS

TABLE *of* CONTENTS

SECTION 1: YOU ARE NOT ALONE

SECTION 2: NAVIGATING THE JOURNEY

DEDICATION

———

IN MEMORY OF MY LATE WIFE, VICTORIA. YOU ARE A BEAUTIFUL SOUL who gave so much of yourself to those you loved. Your care and compassion as a wife and mother inspired and awed me every day. I will always remember the laughter we shared and celebrate the fact that you are resting happily in the loving arms of the Lord.

To my son, Andersen, I am proud of the man you are and all that you have overcome. You have inspired me to share our journey to help others find the joy we have been blessed to discover along the way.

For those who have struggled or are currently struggling with loss, this is for you. You are *not* alone.

FOREWORD

*W*HEN I FIRST MET MARK IT WAS CLEAR HE WAS DIFFERENT. WARM and charismatic, his sense of humor and love of life were evident. I liked him immediately. On that first encounter we shared life-story snapshots and how our journeys had led us to the Nashville area. As the conversation progressed, I was surprised with the comfort and peace he exhibited while opening up about the heartbreaking loss of his wife two and a half years prior. The most interesting aspect of that discussion was the transparency and tenderness with which he recounted what was clearly a traumatic event. Although the sparkle in his eyes remained, tears appeared and the story he shared captivated me both personally and professionally.

As a healthcare professional I have encountered many people who have suffered loss. I work directly with clients who are struggling with psychiatric and mental health challenges as part of my job as a board certified nurse practitioner. My career has reinforced the reality that life can be hard, and the toll that loss can take is oftentimes overwhelming. Many are struggling with related emotional pain that paralyzes their ability to move forward and reengage life in a positive way. I can relate to this personally as I experienced the painful loss of my father to alcoholism while in my early thirties. While that was a hard time for me, it also inspired me to be particularly sensitive and empathetic to the challenges related to loss.

Mark's mission related to Survive-Alive-Thrive™ was compelling to me on several levels. I was inspired by the fact he was engaged, *immersed* really, in a quest to provide others with insights and strategies to help navigate their journey through loss and emotional brokenness. In the spirit of full transparency, that interest led us into a dating relationship, and a year and a half later we were married. Thus, I am writing this foreword about the work of a man who is now my husband. While I may have an understandable bias, I am compelled to encourage you to take your time with this book both from professional and personal perspectives. It is my belief it will help you as it has me.

To put this in context, six short weeks after our wedding we received an early morning call from the emergency room. My mother, 85 years old, had suffered a terrible fall in the middle of the night. After being transported by helicopter to Vanderbilt Hospital, the severity of her injuries left us with a dire diagnosis. As we were well into the COVID-19 pandemic, we had limited options beyond emergency care. Exceeding her doctor's expectations, Mom was regaining cognitive function and within a few days we had a decision to make. A window had opened for her transfer and we elected to move her from the hospital into our newlywed home to be supported by hospice care. Six days later, she passed away in our guest bedroom.

In the chaos I found peace in the ability to be by her side and provide love and support. I was intimately involved with her care, coordinated family visits, and found peace in the fact she was surrounded by those she loved. In a series of unexpected blessings, as the family matriarch Mom was able to give poignant gifts of love and support while also providing directions and instructions we were expected to follow. (That was so Mom!) It remains a source of comfort that just weeks prior my mother had been able to attend our home-based wedding in the same home in which she passed, a gift for which I remain grateful.

As you may know, hospice is a 24-hour commitment and can be exhausting. During that time, Mark and I shared many deep and intimate conversations related to what we were facing. Losing my mother was painful for me, and we spent many hours talking through our current situation and exploring insights gained from his journey and from those shared by others. Those talks were essentially a walk through the foundations of this book. In another example of God's perfect timing, the years Mark had invested writing and developing the Survive-Alive-Thrive model were enormously helpful to me when I needed it most. In the same way, it is my hope and prayer that his book will serve to help you navigate your journey through loss on the way to finding hope, healing, and a joy-filled life.

From a mental health caregiver perspective, I would like to encourage you to lean in and carefully consider many of the healthy steps shared throughout the Survive, Alive, and Thrive chapters in section 2. There are many valuable recommendations related to healthy living including eating well, exercising, maintaining sleep routines, and personal organization. Such steps are important for maintaining ongoing good mental health and are particularly critical when going through the trauma of a personal loss.

As someone who has been through loss, it's my hope you will also be inspired to embrace your family, to forgive and accept forgiveness, and to reach out to those who need your support. Relationships are so crucial in times of loss that *now* is the time to be intentional about making friends, developing a meaningful social circle, and being a good friend to others. Don't wait. We all enjoy life more fully when it's shared with others, and those relationships are invaluable when we need them the most.

Finally, please be gentle with yourself and others. As the uplifting, final section of this book is entitled "Greater Than That," I am thankful to be reminded that God is greater than any difficulty we can experience and is always with us when we need Him the most. He loves us unconditionally and sees us as only our Creator can, providing grace and forgiveness when we need it the most. It's from that gift He inspires us to provide the same grace to others that we have been blessed to receive ourselves.

Melyn

Dr. M. Melyn Galbreath
MSN, RN, FNP-BC, PMHNP-BC

INTRODUCTION

*I*F YOU HAVE PICKED UP THIS BOOK IT'S LIKELY THAT YOU, A LOVED one, or someone you care about has experienced loss and brokenness. It's not *just because* you picked up this book that this statement is likely true; it's because we *all* go through loss and brokenness in some way along our life journey. While most of us have consoled or felt sympathy and empathy for someone who has gone through such an experience, when you go through it yourself, it's different. This has happened to you. Your life has been devastated, and your world turned upside down. I know this because I'm right there with you. I've been through it more than once. These experiences are woven into the fabric of my life story.

If you've lost someone you love who was an integral part of your daily life to illness or a life-altering tragedy, I've been there. Perhaps you've been diagnosed with cancer, a tumor, or another devastating illness. I can relate as I've sat with the doctor who looked me in the eye and shared the shocking diagnosis that I had cancer. You or someone you love may be fighting or struggling with mental illness, depression, PTSD, or another socially and culturally isolating and stigmatized illness or disorder. I understand what that's like after having spent 10 years caring for family members suffering from clinical depression and other mental health challenges. These are some of the "big ones," but in this broken world there are many experiences with which we struggle that lead to brokenness, including divorce, financial catastrophe, loss of a job and career setbacks, drug and alcohol addictions, and more. These are all examples of different types of losses.

So what do we do in these circumstances? This book is intended provide a road map to help you navigate your journey, and to show you that there is hope and the opportunity to find joy on the other side of your loss. Most importantly, I want to assure you that you're not alone in this journey.

What Makes this Book Different?

I am not a doctor. I don't have a degree in psychology and have never practiced as a social worker. I am not a pastor, priest, rabbi, or self-professed healer or religious leader. So who am I? I'm like you and so many others, just a guy who has attempted to walk life's gauntlet of trials and tribulations while riding the roller coaster of ups and downs, victories and setbacks. Along the way, I was given a very special gift and direction to share it with others so they could experience the same.

But this is not just about my journey—it's about *millions* of us who have experienced loss and brokenness. This book is written from the perspective of those of us who have *been through loss ourselves,* providing insight from some who have experienced healed hearts as well as from those who are still in the battle. Over the past five years I have committed my life to this task, leading grief groups, speaking with hundreds of people about their stories, and formally interviewing dozens on the paths to better understanding and sharing how the grieving and healing process works. I remain engaged in that process today and consider it a privilege.

Who does this impact? According to a *WebMD* survey in 2019,[1] more than 71 percent of Americans were directly affected by some form of loss over the previous three years—that's more than 200 million of us . . . and that survey was generated *before* the COVID-19 pandemic. The bottom line is that the numbers are staggering and many of us are struggling.

---

1 *WebMD* Survey footnote: "The Grief Experience: Survey Shows It's Complicated." By Debbie Koenig, July 11, 2019. Survey taken May 16 – May 19, 2019. https:// www.webmd.com/special-reports/grief-stages/20190711/the-grief-experience-survey-shows-its-complicated

What to Expect in this Book

Survive-Alive-Thrive™ is a new model for understanding and navigating the grief journey. If you've ever been to a mall, you're familiar with the kiosk maps that say, "You Are Here." In much the same way, Survive-Alive-Thrive will provide you with a better understanding of where you are in your journey and help you experience healing with less stress and anxiety along the way. Importantly, although each of our loss experiences is uniquely personal and different, we also share many common responses. Through the process of sharing experiences with others, I've been able to identify, chart, and provide hallmarks that are common and relatable to each of us. It's my hope that with this knowledge, you will recognize your place on the map and be reassured that you are not alone in your experience.

Each chapter is followed by questions to stimulate thought and reflection. They are also intended to serve as a guide for group discussions within community and church groups that strive to build deeper and more intimate friendships. While these conversations can sometimes be uncomfortable, there is great opportunity for building meaningful relationships when sharing our stories of loss and brokenness. As an added benefit, the mere act of sharing can be healing.

For those who have not yet experienced loss and may know someone who has, I've also provided insights on how to support others who are going through the grieving process. It's amazing how so many us don't know what to say to comfort a friend, and we inadvertently make matters worse with the best of intentions. Think of this as a helpful book of tips and insights to help others as well as to prepare yourself for the future.

Finally, as one who is grateful for a relationship with God and Jesus, section 3 is dedicated to the critical role that faith plays in having the hope and confidence that you can find happiness, regardless of what life puts in our path. It's been my experience that when we are in direct relationship with God, that living a joy-filled life is directly tied to His love and grace.

Thanks for reading, and God bless you.

PREFACE

———

MY HAND REACHED FOR THE CELL PHONE CHARGING ON MY NIGHT-stand. It was 3:19 a.m. I rolled over and buried my face in my pillow, praying for just a little more sleep—my only defense against the onslaught of images that had occupied every corner of my mind for the past week. But sleep was no longer an option as the memories mercilessly flooded over me again. My wife's lifeless body. The look of shock and fear on my son's face as he backed out of the doorway, unable to process the scene before him. The time spent on my hands and knees, crawling around the garage floor like a wounded animal.

A new day had begun . . . whether I was ready for it or not.

I felt the tears welling and grabbed my phone to see how long I'd delayed the inevitable. 3:32 a.m. I'd put it off thirteen minutes this time. *A little better today*, I thought, as I sat up and swung my legs off the side of the bed. My body reacted to the now-familiar posture, and I began to weep. Softly. Mournfully. I glanced over my shoulder at the undisturbed pillow and blankets on the other side of the bed. The sweet smile and gentle touch that had greeted me most mornings for the past two decades were gone.

I prayed a simple prayer, thanking God for walking with me on this unexpected journey. That brought some peace, but my mind was already racing. I needed to process.

It was still dark outside, a good two hours before the late-May sun rose over New Canaan, Connecticut.

Time to go for a walk.

I was alone.

YOU ARE
— —
NOT
— —
ALONE

Chapter 1

LIFE, LOVE, AND FAITH

————

PERHAPS LIKE YOU, LIFE'S JOURNEY HAS CHALLENGED ME IN WAYS I never could have imagined. I've endured significant losses and periods of brokenness that have tested me and brought me to my knees along the way. Losses I never *wanted* to bear. Losses I never thought I'd *be able* to bear. It's funny how we never think we can do the impossible …until the impossible *arrives* and we're forced to deal with it. For me, that impossible moment was the death of my wife in 2016. For you, it might be the loss of a child or parent, a serious or terminal medical diagnosis, depression or another mental health condition, a broken relationship, the news that your child has special needs, a financial crisis, or something else entirely. Having personally experienced each of these challenges, I have also had the opportunity to spend over one thousand hours of one-on-one time with others who have experienced their own loss and brokenness, battled through adversity, and survived to find hope and happiness again.

The purpose of this book is to share my story and provide insights gained from my experiences and those shared by others.

Together, we will explore the unique nature of different loss experiences, as well as their similarities. I have included recovery steps and strategy examples that have led to healing and happiness for those who have been or are currently going through similar challenges. Importantly, these insights are not from third-party doctor's or therapist's patient files, but from those of us who have been through it ourselves, from those with whom I've engaged in face-to-face interviews and discussions over the past four years. I'll introduce a new model called Survive-Alive-Thrive™ that reframes how we understand and experience trauma and loss, while providing navigation strategies for finding hope and happiness along the journey. Most of all, I hope to make it clear to you that you are *not* alone.

But first, to help you better understand where we're going, I'd like to share with you where I've been.

A Brief Backstory

Growing up in the '60s in a modest ranch-style home in the northern suburbs of Chicago, my early childhood is best described as simple and safe, with a stay-at-home mom and a white-collar father who worked in marketing. Through the somewhat rose-colored glasses of a boy's memory, it was a story of the American dream with parents who had met in college, married shortly after graduating, and quickly produced two boys, my younger brother coming almost three years after I was born.

Family get-togethers with the neighbors and their kids were a routine weekend activity, and by middle school, I was consumed with sports, including the local swimming team, community baseball leagues, and hockey played in the bitter cold on outdoor ice rinks in Chicago. We attended an Episcopal church most Sundays, where I listened to sermons and went through rituals, most of which I did not relate to or understand.

It was a tumultuous time for the country, with historic benchmark events taking place, such as the Cuban Missile Crisis, JFK's assassination, Martin Luther King Jr.'s "I Have a Dream" speech, the Vietnam War, and the hippie movement, to name a few. That said, as a grade-school kid, it was fairly simple. My goals were to have fun with neighborhood kids, make the sports teams I tried out for, and get good grades to keep my parents happy. It was an idyllic youth in the midst of a world in perpetual chaos.

My sister was born when I was almost eight, and a few years later, our parents moved us to a larger home in a suburb thirty minutes away to accommodate our growing family. By the time I was in high school, it was clear that my parents' marriage was struggling. My mother started working, my dad traveled a lot for work, and things were going sideways for our idyllic suburban family. I was fortunate to be a decent student and a four-season athlete, which kept me somewhat grounded. But I was a rebellious teenager, and when dreams of playing a sport in college were dashed with a series of knee injuries, I became more free-spirited and pushed back on authority.

When my father made it clear that if I wanted to attend college, I would have to find a way to pay my tuition, I did. Combining student loans with in-semester part-time jobs and full-time summer employment was an eye-opening experience. After a summer spent driving a combine, harvesting beans and peas in the fields of rural Illinois, I entered my junior year lacking direction. To make matters worse, I was unsure how I would pay for the next semester's tuition. But then a solution presented itself: a local steel manufacturing facility near my college campus was hiring entry-level manual labor for the night shift. It was the lowest level job in the place but lucrative; that is, if you could handle the role and work the hours. I applied and was hired, dropped out of college, and spent the next eighteen months unloading steel off an assembly line—steel that had just come from the mouth of a 1,200-degree furnace. It was a brutal and phys- ically demanding job with twelve-hour-long shifts, six days a week, and it was mercilessly hot in the summer. The pay was good, though, combining overtime and a six-day work week, and the experience taught me many life lessons about responsibility, accountability, and perseverance that were hard-learned in the crucible of independent financial survival. It was a turning point in my life.

Adversity became an ally and a motivator. I was driven by the challenge to overcome and relished the belief that it would either kill me or I would emerge a stronger man. I used my perceived plight as motivation, like Lieutenant Dan in *Forrest Gump* who defiantly yells at God from atop his boat in a raging storm, "You call this a storm?!" It was my rallying cry against the challenges of a life that I felt were beating me down and trying to break me.

I returned to college eighteen months later, highly motivated and grateful to be attending classes again. Pouring myself into my studies (imagine that!), the next two years went quickly. I excelled academically and received recognition for work I was doing in the radio-TV-film department, landing a prime-time radio host role on the campus station. Receiving my diploma in 1981 was a special accomplishment that I still appreciate and value today.

I accepted a late-night radio host job in the Chicago market immediately out of school, teeing up prerecorded content and reading news and weather. With substantial student loans to repay, I quickly realized I needed a higher paying job. Grad school would have to come later, if at all. I submitted numerous job applications, taking the first corporate sales position I was offered. I then spent the next few years in traveling sales roles, climbing the so-called "prove-it ladder" and moving around the country covering a variety of assigned territories.

In 1985, having relocated to the Chicago area for a new sales position, I learned that my mother's kidney disease had progressed and that both her kidneys needed to be removed. The surgeries would leave her 100 percent reliant on dialysis, as well as on a donor waiting list. It was a serious situation, and with my sister studying abroad and my brother stationed in Germany, I moved into her home to provide care and support.

To my surprise, spending the next year living with and getting to know my mother as an adult was one of the great blessings of my life. She had earned her master's degree and Series 7 securities credentials after she and my dad divorced—while raising my younger siblings and coping with the pain of frequent dialysis without complaint or resentment. I learned a great deal about character, resilience, and determination in our year together, and we became closer than I could ever have imagined.

Following her first surgery, I sat in the ICU and wept, quietly contemplating the possibility that she might not survive. To our family's great joy and relief, the surgeries were successful, and she received a donor kidney that blessed her with renewed health and freedom from dialysis.

A year later, I moved back out on my own and was enjoying success selling advertising space in magazines. The industry was challenging and competitive, and my life was busy with traveling for work. But while it was fun being single in my twenties, I felt something was missing, a feeling that that there must be more to life than making money and pursuing adventure. Little did I know that my longings would be answered 2,500 miles west of California in the middle of the Pacific Ocean.

A Love Story

It was a match made in paradise. The year was 1987, and I was a twenty-nine-year-old magazine sales executive with management aspirations. My boss had unexpectedly dropped out of a business trip to Hawaii, rewarding me with the opportunity to fill in for him at a direct-marketing trade show in Waikiki. Single and almost thirty, I'd been in several relationships but had started wondering if I'd ever find *the one*—my soul mate. Then there she was, standing in front of my booth on the showroom floor. She was in Hawaii on behalf of her Manhattan-based publishing company, trying to get publicity from a magazine I represented. It was all I could do to maintain a sense of professionalism. Victoria was stunning, funny, demure, and wickedly smart. Her rapid-fire wit and good humor kept me on my toes in that first encounter, and I immediately knew I wanted *more* encounters with this intriguing woman.

As the week progressed, I convinced her to join me and a small group of colleagues for a sunset cruise along the shores of Waikiki. For her, this was strictly business. For me, not so much. We had a great time on the cruise, but it was later, when the group ended the night at the hotel's beachfront terrace, that I saw the qualities that made her special. Watching her interact with others, seeing her uncanny empathy on display as she patiently listened to a colleague talk about his recent breakup . . . I was smitten. I sent her flowers the next day and tried to spend every moment I could with her during the rest of the conference. When I learned she had already planned a post-conference extended stay on the island to relax and recharge, I did the same. With the trade show behind us, we shared a tropical adventure, snorkeling, visiting other islands, climbing recently cooled volcano flows, and discovering hidden watering holes along black-sand beaches. By the end of that second week, I was full-on, head-over-heels in love with her.

I lived in Chicago at the time and she was based in New York City. That gave us a safe distance from which to get to know each other over the next year. We saw each other whenever we could, often finagling our business trips to coincide so we could meet up in different places across the country. We enjoyed several weekend getaways. It was a fairytale romance where every time we saw each other, we were in a different city.

A year later, when a career opportunity gave me the chance to move to Manhattan, I jumped at it. After twelve long months of long-distance dating, we'd finally be in the same city. With that move, our relationship was officially *on the clock*.

During this time, I discovered how Victoria's childhood had impacted her life. Her father tragically died in a car accident when she was just ten. That loss emotionally broke her mother, Cathy, who had suffered a history of postpartum depression following the birth of several of her seven children, all born before she was twenty-five. In an act of desperation, Cathy, now a widow, moved the family to a pseudo-Christian (and cultish) commune in central Florida. It was a shocking change for the family, as any sense of security was lost. Two years later, Cathy met and married a new resident of the community and they escaped "the Farm" in the middle of the night to move to Long Island, New York. Victoria, just entering seventh grade, was now forced to acclimate to the rugged social jungle of Long Island's teenage landscape. Her life felt completely upside down. It was a long way from the more rural settings of south Florida and a completely different world from the communal environment they had just left.

Her new stepfather—a Vietnam veteran with PTSD—was physically and emotionally abusive, and Victoria ultimately moved out of the family home at age sixteen, living with friends and then returning to the South to finish high school in Mississippi. These experiences left her with a deep-rooted need for independence and self-sufficiency. It also deeply affected her ability to trust others—including romantic partners.

Our fast-moving careers made it easy for us to keep busy when we were not together. Victoria was committed to her career and growing success, managing her publishing company's newly emerging digital data group. I wanted more from our relationship, but she was unable—personally and professionally—to formally commit.

After eighteen months in Manhattan, I was offered a promotion that would require a move back to Chicago to manage the company's Midwest sales office and operation. At the same time, Victoria's employer decided to move her division to Tampa, Florida, and asked her to relocate and continue managing her group. After several agonizing discussions, I took the job in Chicago, and she took the job in Florida. It felt like our love affair was over.

Less than a year later, unhappy with the new Florida-based operations and management structure, Victoria resigned and joined me in Chicago. She was exhausted from the Florida experience, fighting chronic fatigue, and in desperate need of some rest and recuperation. It had been an unsteady ride, but we were together, we were committed, and we were happy. Within a year, the company for which I had moved back to Chicago restructured its management. Changes were in the air, and the entrepreneurial spirit called. In 1990 I left the company, and Victoria and I started an event-marketing business together with venture capital and media support from a division of 3M. We called it ViMark—a combination of our names. This was an all-new and rewarding adventure for us, and we learned a great deal about running a business (and about each other) in the process. After working elbow to elbow together for two years filled with highs and lows, our young business needed a capital infusion. Exhausted from the stress of running a startup together, we decided to re-assess our relationship and take a break to think things over. I continued to manage the business while Victoria returned to New York to care for her mother, who was going through a family health crisis. Again, the future of our relationship was up in the air.

Six months after Victoria returned to New York, I received an unexpected job offer with a New York magazine publisher while in the process of raising incremental operating funds for ViMark. It was 1993—five years into our up-and-down relationship—and I put it all on the line. With ring in hand, I got down on my knees and asked Victoria to marry me. I wanted to take the job in Manhattan and move with her to the Connecticut suburbs to start a family. We were both in our mid-thirties at that point, and it was time for us to either invest fully into this relationship or move on.

To my great joy, she said yes! After spending a lifetime carefully guarding her heart, she was ready to place her trust in a partner for life. It was an honor and a joy being the person with whom she felt safe and loved enough to trust with her hopes, dreams, hurts, and fears. We eloped in 1995 while on a scuba-diving trip. On Thanksgiving, we were married at sunset on the beach in Cozumel. In 1996, we bought a charming stone home in the Connecticut suburbs with three rolling acres of property and a creek running through the back yard.

Victoria was the missing piece I'd longed for, a partner I loved deeply, and we were excited to start our new life together as husband and wife. Our puzzle was still one piece short, but that was filled in October 1996 when our son, Andersen, was born—just eleven months after our Thanksgiving nuptials in Mexico. I had recently been promoted and was in the middle of what would be a seven-year daily commute from the picturesque neighborhoods of Connecticut to the big-city business life of New York City. With a loving wife, a beautiful baby boy, an exciting career . . . I was living the American dream!

So why wasn't I happy?

Wait, What? Why Does God Matter?

Do you know what it's like to get nearly everything you ever wanted in life yet still feel a strange hole in your heart? That's where I was in 1999 at forty-one years old. We were building a wonderful life, but it was strangely . . . unfulfilling. There was a haunting feeling of "this is not enough" that compelled me forward. I kept throwing whatever I could into that void in my soul—money, toys, parties, promotions, accolades, houses, vacations—but nothing seemed to fill it. And it was driving me (and Victoria) to the brink.

An encounter with a new neighbor brought all this hidden frustration and dissatisfaction to a head—turning my worldview upside down. Victoria and I were on a walk through the neighborhood with two-year-old Andersen when we passed a moving truck parked in front of a nearby home. As we walked by, a young woman darted out to introduce herself. Trish and her husband, Steve, were moving in and welcomed us into their home. I immediately liked them both. Steve was a warm, welcoming guy with a sense of personal peace and a self-deprecating sense of humor. After a little chitchat, he explained that he was a graphic designer by trade, but he had just started a new ministry career with a church in town.

Cue my red flags.

Steve never pressed the issue, though. In fact, I was the one who brought it up when I saw him the following week. We hung out for a while before I bluntly said, "Okay, man. Do me a favor. Give me your best Jesus pitch, and let's get this over with."

He just laughed. "You know, Mark, you seem like you have a pretty good life," he said. "In my experience, happy and successful people who are enjoying life rarely start looking to God for answers unless something goes wrong. If your situation changes, though, let me know. Otherwise, I just thought we could be friends."

"Well . . . good," I said. "Because you're right. I *am* happy. I'm *really, really happy.*" I heard it in my voice, though—some weird need to *convince* Steve I was truly happy. That got stuck in my mind like a splinter under a fingernail. A few days later, seemingly out of nowhere, I turned to Victoria and asked, "We're happy . . . right?"

She took a breath and looked me in the eye. "Not completely," she said quietly. After a brief pause, she continued, "I don't know if we want the same things out of life and for our family." Her response caught me off guard. In the two years following our son's birth, we were growing apart on the issue of faith. We had talked about it in the context of our parental approach and strategy for exposing Andersen to religion, but Victoria was now explicitly expressing her concern about how it was impacting our relationship and future. She felt the same spiritual emptiness and dissatisfaction I did but wanted to look to God for answers. My resistance was dividing us, and we were at the point where I had to admit that the path I was on wasn't bringing me happiness. I couldn't keep doing the same things the same way if I wanted a different outcome for myself and our family. It was time for me to take a serious look at God and reflect on how my views about Jesus Christ had developed and evolved.

I called Steve and asked if he could meet me for a chat. On the agenda was how God could matter in a practical sense. What difference would a change in view make to me as a husband and father, as well as in my career? When we met at a local restaurant, he listened to my story and suggested I take a fresh look at the concept of religion vs. faith. I'd always conflated the two, and my view was that *religion* represented two thousand years of judgementalism, political maneuvering, and corporate church hypocrisy. *Faith*, however, seemed to be a simpler concept about having a *friendship with God* . . . like He was there to talk to and know personally. These are obviously very different concepts that I needed to spend time on and potentially reevaluate.

For me, the critical issue came down to a question my brother had once asked me in a debate about faith and theology. "If your view is not Christian, that's your choice. But what do you do about the historical question of Jesus?" he had proposed. Turns out that trying to answer that question was the dilemma I now faced. It was time for me to try and determine if the ministry of Jesus as told by the apostles was historically accurate or the inspiring story of a good man that had been distorted and exaggerated by misguided converts. I expanded my reading beyond that of skeptic literature to include authors who offered insights and facts I could understand on both sides of the argument. After much research, prayer, and reflection, my conclusion was that the narratives of the New Testament were true. As the faith journey is personal for each of us, this part of my story is not intended as an apologetics debate. Instead, my goal is to share how my personal experiences have been impacted by this conclusion and how it can impact your experience with loss and brokenness.

The changes came hard and fast. It was as if I had been walking one direction my entire life and, suddenly, I had done an about-face and started heading in the opposite direction. At the same time, this presented some serious problems in how I lived my life. I knew that, in order to be authentic to my new faith and worldview, many things would have to change. I decided to rethink who I was, how I acted, where I worked, what I cared about, how I prioritized my goals and ambitions, and with whom and how I spent my time. I realized my lack of fulfillment was the result of pursuing the wrong things for the wrong reasons most of my life. If I finally wanted a different outcome, it was time to do things—do *everything*—differently.

I professed Jesus as my Lord and Savior on Thanksgiving Day, 1999, the day of our fourth wedding anniversary, with Andersen now three years old. Within months, Victoria and I were actively praying together and digging into this new view of life as a team. Our new shared passion for God had saved and changed our marriage. It impacted our families, friendships, career, financial goals, how we spent our free time, how we raised our son, and literally every other part of our lives. God had cleaned house inside my heart and mind, totally uprooting my "I'm on my own" worldview and replacing it with a life centered squarely on a personal relationship with God and the idea of grace through Jesus Christ.

In the Gospel of John, Jesus tells his disciples at their last supper together, "I no longer call you servants. . . . Instead, I have called you friends" (John 15:15). I was a new man ... God was my *friend,* and my heart was truly happy for the first time.

No One Ever Promised Me a Rose Garden

While Victoria and I were thrilled with this new underlying foundation for our marriage and family, our life certainly wasn't perfect. Many people think that when you walk with Jesus all your troubles will be over, but that has not been my experience. That being said, it has made an immeasurable difference in how I've been able to understand and cope with the adversity that life has thrown my way.

In fact, my first experience with loss as a Christian came on February 2, 2000, three short months after my declaration of faith, when I received a call that my mother had experienced a heart attack and was on the way to the hospital. She would never regain consciousness. She was gone, and it was a crushing loss. In the midst of her loss, I was given a remarkable gift, having written her a letter the day she died and mailed it to her before I received the news. When I arrived in Chicago to meet with my siblings to mourn, reflect, and plan her memorial service, there it was, sitting in her incoming mail. Although my mom wouldn't have the chance to read it here on earth, it was a comforting gift to me to have expressed my love and appreciation for her role in my life before I learned the Lord had taken her home. As a result, I urge everyone reading this to sit down *right now* and write a letter to someone you love and appreciate. Tell them you love them. You will never regret it.

My new understanding of God's love freed me to join my siblings as we hosted a celebratory memorial service focused on Mom's remarkable life and those she had touched. We were *sure* that she was with God, no longer physically suffering, and rejoicing in the grace of Jesus's love. In the context of my question to Steve about how a relationship with God could make a difference in my "real life," I was seeing this play out right before my eyes. I realized that my new Christ-centered worldview had changed everything about losing someone I loved, and I needed to share that experience.

Returning to Connecticut, I resolved to start a men's group at our home church, and it quickly started to grow and gain popularity. The focus was not on Bible study per se, but on the difference it makes in life to actually know Jesus *as a friend*. What I found was that while many of us struggle with the idea and experiences we associate with religion, we long for a God-centered spiritual relationship that actually makes a difference in our lives. Jesus had become the touchstone of my life and it had been life-changing for me, and I'm grateful to have made many close friends— brothers, really—through that process.

The Path Ahead Gets Bumpy

The next decade was an exciting time. I joined a local Connecticut online marketing startup that rescued me from seven years of riding Metro-North trains into New York City and replaced those with a fifteen-minute local commute. Little did I know that startup would push through early challenges and explode with success, taking my career and income to new heights. Now working so close to home, I was able to coach youth soccer and hockey, become active in additional ministry initiatives, and agree to chair the board of a faith-based nonprofit in Manhattan that ran the East Harlem Little League. Victoria and I partnered in serving in various ways within the community. Life was busy and full.

While we were enjoying business and financial success and had developed several wonderful friendships, we still faced plenty of heartache and anxieties. Some of those were centered on our son. Once he started preschool, it became clear that Andersen had unique challenges for which we weren't prepared. He was a smart kid, yet some things were clearly different in how he processed them compared to his peers. After what seemed like endless testing, he was diagnosed with various language-based learning differences, dyslexia being the easiest to identify.

His frustration with school and social situations—not to mention the bullying and stigmatizing that are thrust upon children with these issues—led him to act out in various ways. It hit us hard when our local preschool effectively kicked him out. Andersen was not yet four. It was painful and traumatic for Victoria, and I was appalled at their tone-deaf decision. The social shaming had begun, and we would learn that this was going to be a long-term struggle.

In public grade school, his teachers didn't know how to teach him or how to handle him, and it sometimes seemed like the entire school district was against us. After a particularly troubling event in second grade, we had no choice but to hire attorneys, advocates, and other resources to demand that the district comply with the state's requirements to provide appropriate educational resources under the Americans with Disabilities Act. While we prevailed with a favorable ruling and received the financial support for Andersen's education, it was a traumatic and emotional experience. Throw in the nightmare of working with pediatric neurologists, behaviorists, and psychologists who specialized in testing medications and other methods to try and help our son, and you end up with one very stressed family.

This is a painful situation for many, many families and something most people don't seem comfortable discussing. That leaves many of us struggling, isolated, stigmatized, and alone. The good news is that we discovered many great organizations and resources that were willing to support us. If you are struggling with a child with learning differences, I urge you to reach out to someone for help.

While our marriage was truly tested as we navigated Andersen's challenges (a stunning percentage of marriages with special-needs children end in divorce), Victoria and I never lost sight of what we were fighting for, and we tried to avoid turning our frustrations on each other. We were a team. It was tough, but I couldn't imagine doing any of this without her.

That is, until I almost lost her.

QUESTIONS FOR DISCUSSION

1. Something led you to pick up this book. Whether you bought it for your-self or someone else bought it because they thought you needed it, here we are. As we get started on this journey, take a few moments to articulate why this book is important to you, and why it is important *now*.

2. Has there been a time in your life when everything *seemed* perfect, yet you felt like something important was missing? How did you handle it? Looking back, what do you think was missing?

3. Do you have a friend, family member, or influential relationship who acted as your "Steve," leading you to a deeper relationship with God? Can you describe that experience?

4. Throughout this book, we'll be discussing the importance of our personal histories, something I'll call "backstories" later on. Take a moment now to reflect on where you came from. How do you think your backstory shapes how you approach loss and heartache?

5. How has faith impacted your life experiences up to this point? What does faith mean to you?

Chapter 2

THE BUMPY ROAD

—

I IGNORED THE CALL FOR A SECOND TIME AS I SAT IN A MANAGE-
ment meeting on a September afternoon in 2010. I didn't recognize
the number and my team was busy prepping for an upcoming board
meeting. "Spam calls …," I murmured to myself. As my cell phone vibrated
a third time in less than a minute, I took the call, turning away from the
conference table at which we were all circled. "Who is this?" I demanded
in a hushed and somewhat annoyed tone. "I am a paramedic," the voice on
the line explained, "and I am in the ambulance with your wife."

As I instinctively jumped to my feet, colleagues eyed me with curi-
osity. "Ambulance!?" I said loudly, trying to process his words. The conference room went silent as everyone stopped to listen. As I walked out, the
EMS technician calmly and patiently tried to explain that Victoria had
been in a serious car accident, was on her way to the hospital, and was
fortunate to be alive. If you've ever been on the receiving end of a phone
call like this, you know the strange mix of panic, fear, and confusion that
immediately swept over me. Those feelings got worse when I passed her
vehicle on the way to hospital. The crash site was on the route I was taking,

and our totaled SUV was in a heap on the side of the road. As I passed by, all I could think was, *How could anyone survive this type of accident?* It was shocking and unsettling, but the paramedic said she was going to survive. I prayed as I sped to the ER. This was new territory, and I was scared.

Seeing Victoria was an unexpected relief. Her face was bruised and she was in a neck brace, but she looked great compared to what I had imagined she would look like after seeing our vehicle. She was drugged, foggy, and sore from the impact. "What happened?" she asked. "I don't know," I said, "but thank God you're okay." It was all I could think to say as I fought back tears. After a week at home recovering, her physical bruising was improving but the discomfort wasn't, and she started having some new and troubling symptoms. It was becoming evident that the accident had resulted in head and neck trauma and that neurological damage was causing symptoms that would come and go, making life miserable for Victoria.

Although her symptoms were often more annoying than painful, they were always lurking, and she knew they could come upon her at any time. We spent several months visiting different doctors and desperately searching for relief. Various neurologists and specialists focused on short-term solutions, offering limited treatment options. And although we were fortunate to have access to highly competent medical care, her doctors could not identify the specific cause of Victoria's discomfort and were unable to offer effective solutions for relief, let alone produce a path to full recovery. Needless to say, it was incredibly frustrating for us both. Moving forward bravely and with resolve, Victoria found comfort focusing on her faith, family, and helping others in need. Still, it was an ongoing struggle, as she battled symptoms we could not seem to adequately address.

We marched on with our lives and in 2011, after eleven exciting and rewarding years with my job at the marketing firm, I left the comfort of a well-paid management role to launch a technology-based digital film production company. At the same time, we were in the early stages of a remodeling project for our home that Victoria primarily managed.

Andersen was applying to a boarding high school that specializes in educating intelligent kids with learning differences; if accepted, he would be attending in the fall of 2012. These time demands added stress to our lives and took their toll on Victoria.

Over the next year, I watched helplessly as Victoria became increasingly depressed—a natural response, I thought, to the pain and aggravation she experienced daily. However, unbeknownst to me, Victoria had also started a private battle with paranoia and delusional thinking, meaning she sometimes couldn't tell what was real and what wasn't. While her more obvious physiological struggles were apparent to me, the wheels came off in May 2012, when she called me while I was on the way to drop off a few thank-you teacher gifts at our son's middle school. In a panic, she asked me to turn around and come home because, she explained, the FBI, some parents, and school officials were conspiring against me and waiting to take me into custody.

At first, I thought she was joking. She wasn't.

When I got home, she led us out of our kitchen to the back yard to talk—because she was convinced our house was bugged as part of the conspiracy. As I was confronted with her psychological break, it was clear to me that her mental health battle was far more serious than I realized.

With recommendations from friends and our pastor, we were fortunate to meet with a psychiatrist the very next day. Following a generous two-hour meeting and evaluation session, the doctor pulled me aside to explain that Victoria was experiencing delusions and paranoia as part of a clinical depression related to her brain injury and also likely tied to genetic and family history. She continued by saying Victoria was at high risk for suicide, needed to be medicated, and should be admitted to a mental-health treatment facility immediately for her protection. I will tell you right now, nothing can ever prepare a spouse for that news.

I asked my mother-in-law to come to Connecticut and stay with us while we addressed this crisis, as she had a history of battling depression and I hoped that she could relate to and comfort her daughter in ways I was unable to. As we gently explained the doctor's recommendation, Victoria tearfully and emotionally expressed her fears as well as her desire not to go into a treatment facility. After prayer and reflection, despite the doctor's recommendation, I agreed not to force her admittance to a local mental-health facility and arranged what I considered to be around-the-clock supervision for her at home. With our psychiatrist's and psychologist's supervision, she started medication immediately, and I arranged for twice weekly doctor meetings and assessments. Victoria's mother, Cathy, moved in with us, and we worked out a schedule where Victoria was never left alone. It was an emotionally challenging, unrelenting demand on all of us, but we had to try to make it work for Victoria's sake.

It took months to find the right mix of medications that allowed Victoria to be alert and not feel like a zombie, while also allowing her to sort through the confusion and delusions that she was battling. If you have been through a mental health crisis with someone you love, you can understand the difficulty of dealing with an invisible enemy. Further, it's a socially stigmatizing health condition and many people have strong opinions on the subject of mental illness. During this time, some people chose to share their personal views and beliefs about depression, which I will kindly characterize as misguided attempts to try and help. These are hurtful things to hear from people who have never dealt with the struggles of mental health but feel free to offer their theories, nonetheless. The reality is that finding mental health caretakers is expensive and difficult. Insurance management is a nightmare. Battling social stigma and ignorance is brutal and unforgiving. If you are facing this challenge, I strongly encourage you to connect with others who understand how daunting this struggle can be. You can find resources and connections on the resources tab of our website.

Thankfully, after two years' time, life began to look somewhat normal. Victoria was taking her medication, had responded to her treatment, was receiving ongoing counseling, and, other than a few odd conversations, gave many of our friends little external indication that anything was different. By the end of 2014—four years following her 2010 car accident and two and a half years after engaging psychiatric support—things felt like we were back on the right track. It had been such a struggle, requiring patience, support, and love. Victoria's faith in Christ kept her grounded when she was feeling vulnerable to her disease, and worship and prayer assured her of God's presence and brought comfort only He can provide.

Surely, we were through the worst, we both hoped and prayed.

Sorry, There's Nothing We Can Do

The years we spent battling Victoria's mental illness were taxing and exhausting. It was a blessing that our son was away at school for many of his mother's toughest seasons. We timed our visits carefully, the medications were working for her, and we enjoyed holidays and breaks as a family that were both healing and comforting. The investment of time and capital in my start-up venture had yielded an exciting and promising partnership with a national bookselling retailer that had contractually agreed to launch our digital video technology in their largest stores in January 2015. We had invested a great deal of time and capital to customize our solution for their stores and were heading into the Christmas season excited with what the new year would bring.

I received a call from a corporate executive at our partner's company the week after Thanksgiving. The news was hard to believe; they had filed for chapter 11 bankruptcy and been ordered to stop any and all new partnership initiatives until reorganization plans had been approved. The chapter 11 process was projected to be lengthy, and there were no guarantees they would honor our contract when reorganized and moving forward. The words still ring in my ears today: "I'm truly sorry that this has happened, Mark. There is nothing we can do."

Stunned and rocked by this gut-punch, Victoria and I agreed we had no choice but to trust God that we would get through this together. It was a financially painful development, and I had good friends and family who had also invested and needed to be informed. I gathered the board of directors to review financial options and investors weighed in on the choices moving forward. We would effectively be starting over. In the end, it was agreed to dissolve the firm and attempt to liquidate what we could to cover outstanding expenses and the costs of dissolution. If you've lost a job or had a serious financial setback, I'm sure you can relate. People lost their jobs, and it was a devastating holiday for us all, particularly in view of our expectations for the new year.

"No Easy Way to Say This"

The death of a parent. Raising a child with special needs. Nearly losing a spouse in an accident. Dealing with painful, ongoing neurological symptoms. Depression. Delusions. Closing a company over the holidays. While being blessed in many significant areas, our family had run the gauntlet of pain and brokenness over that ten-year period, and I was honestly ready for a break.

That was not, apparently, the plan.

In April 2015, I passed a particularly painful kidney stone and was told I needed additional tests. I got "the call" three days later: "Please bring your wife with you as we go over the results of your biopsy." When we arrived in his office, my doctor looked me in the eye as I held Victoria's hand. He simply said, "There is no easy way to say this. The results are back, they are conclusive, and you have prostate cancer."

Okay, I said to myself, *I have cancer*. Now, *cancer* is a word we hear in social circles, but it still shocks you to the core when you're the one getting the news. My immediate reaction was shock and bewilderment. The news hadn't even settled in when the doctor started listing the treatment options available to consider. He gave me a week to review the options and make a decision but made sure I understood how critical our time frame was: if we acted swiftly, he assured me this wouldn't kill me.

Kill me? Was this actually happening?

Victoria and I discussed it throughout the week. Chemotherapy, radioactive seed therapy, and surgery were all on the table. I received counsel from a small circle of friends and family, some of whom are physicians, but I generally felt a need to keep this private. I later learned that many (if not most) people going through cancer keep it a secret, particularly in the early stages of discovery.

A few days later, I received an afternoon call from my good friend Rob, one of those with whom I had shared the news. He was with his wife, Sarah, and she needed to talk to me. He put her on speaker in their car. She said she didn't want to upset me, but she had just been on a prayer walk and had received a message she needed to share. Curious, I was all ears. "You are going to be okay," she said. "God told me you are going to be healed." I was not sure how to exactly respond to that information, but I was thankful for her prayers and message. Grateful for the encouragement but not sure what to do with it, it was time to discuss it with my wife.

Victoria and I talked about it that night and she wanted details: "Did she say *how* you will be healed? . . . Should we do chemo or surgery?" I obviously did not have any answers, so we called Sarah and discussed it further. No details. No plan. Just the message that I would be healed. "The radiation seeds are the way to go," Victoria matter-of-factly stated after the call. "They're going to work. This is good news." From her view, there was nothing more to discuss.

Six days later, I went to bed on the Thursday night before our scheduled call with the doctor, still unsure about the best path to fight my cancer. I also had an important meeting at work that was on my mind. At 4:00 a.m., I woke up with a start. The room was dark and quiet. Victoria was sound asleep. But for some reason, I woke up on high alert, like something either *was* happening or was *about* to happen. I lay there for a minute or two, trying to get my bearings and listening intently to the quiet house. Something had woken me up, but I had no idea what it was. Then, out of nowhere, I heard a voice clear as a bell:

"You will be healed, and then I will reveal your commission."

I am sleepy, I thought. This was a bit crazy and somewhat hard for me to believe. It sounded like someone was standing beside my bed talking to me. Surprised and a bit confused, I sat up in bed, thinking maybe it was a residual thought from a dream. But then, for a second time, I heard unmistakably:

"You will be healed, and then I will reveal your commission."

Now *that* got me on my feet quickly. On full alert, I hopped out of bed and checked the security system control panel on the wall, making sure there was no one in the house. Nothing. I went into the bathroom and splashed cold water on my face, trying to make sense of it. Now wide awake, I journaled in my home office, paced, and prayed for an hour or so before crawling back into bed at 5:30. Victoria had slept through everything. *Crazy*, I thought. *Just crazy.* I drifted off to sleep and woke up a couple of hours later like nothing had happened. But something *had* happened. There was no doubt. But what to do about it was another story.

That Friday was a big day for me. Not only did I have the treatment decision phone call with my doctor that afternoon at 2:00, but I was also scheduled to present quarterly financials to the board of directors starting at 9:00 that morning. In the shower, though, my day took a turn in an unexpected direction. It's hard to explain, but I felt an overwhelming need to read the book of Acts in the Bible. I'd read it several times, but this was different. I can only describe it as a need I couldn't ignore. It was like that scene in *Close Encounters of the Third Kind*, when Richard Dreyfuss's character is compelled to build structures out of his mashed potatoes. I had no choice.

I texted my CEO and told him something had come up and that I'd be late for our board meeting. He was concerned, and, of course, I couldn't explain *why* I was going to be late; I wasn't sure myself. "Are you okay?"

he texted. "I'll explain later," I responded, not sure that I would be able to when the time came.

I started reading. Chapter 1. Chapter 2. Chapter 3. *Check the clock.* Chapters 4, 5, 6. *Man, Acts is long.* Chapters 7 and 8. *You still there, God?* After reading for an hour or so, I realized the board meeting was about to start. I had no choice but to continue; it was surreal. After another twenty minutes, I arrived at Acts chapter 20, verse 23. Here, the Apostle Paul is about to return to Jerusalem, and his early church friends are trying to talk him out of it because of the dangers that awaited him there. Paul says:

> I only know that in every city the Holy Spirit warns me that prison and hardships are facing me. However, *I consider my life worth nothing to me; my only aim is to finish the race and complete the task the Lord Jesus has given me—the task of testifying to the good news of God's grace.* (Acts 20:23–24, emphasis added)

I read that passage a few more times when it seemed suddenly so clear. What God was telling me became obvious in a way I cannot explain. Going to my knees, I talked to God as I had many times before, conversationally and in friendship and appreciation. "Okay, God, so you're saying You're going to heal me of cancer, and then I need to commit my life to testifying to Your grace in Christ?"

I felt His confirmation.

It was like a covenant I'd read about so often in the Old Testament, but it was here and now. With me.

What do you say to God in that situation? I was definitely *in.* I told Him I'd give my life to testify to His grace in Jesus Christ. And then, I felt Him release me to go to work, like He was saying, "Okay, sounds good. You can go to work now. Have a nice day."

I got to work, did my presentation late, and had lunch. Around 2:00 p.m., the doctor called. "Well, have you decided which route you want to take on this?" he asked. "Is it going to be chemo or seeds or surgery?"

"Uh ... none of the above."

He asked what I meant, and I explained that I wasn't going to do *anything* about the cancer. He was understandably confused. I tried to think of a way to say this without sounding like a kook, but nothing came to mind. So, I told him the truth: "I'm thinking ... healing."

He said, "Oh ... so you mean naturopathically or homeopathically?"

"Ummm. Not really." I hesitated. "I'm thinking . . . God's going to heal me."

My doctor is a good guy, and he was trying to be as accommodating as possible, but I'm sure he thought I'd lost my mind. After a long pause, he insisted on a face-to-face meeting the following Monday. I agreed, we hung up, and I got back to work.

I'd be lying if I said Victoria took the news well. She didn't. She was a faith-filled woman, but she also knew the danger we were facing. After a lot of talking, though, she accepted my decision, and we committed to be faithful to what I knew God had told me to do—with certain conditions. Victoria stressed that we needed to actively monitor my health, which seemed reasonable, and that was that. My mind was made up and she decided to support me within reason. We committed ourselves to praying about it and thanking God for His intervention in my life. Whether the voice that spoke to me was Jesus, an angel, the Holy Spirit, or God Himself was not important to me. "Why me?" was also not important. It was simply about gratitude and trust; no matter how it ended up, I was in His hands and good with that scenario.

The doctor was skeptical. We met weekly at first, ostensibly to monitor my health and measure PSA status, but his goal was to guide me to a medical solution. When my position did not change, we went to biweekly and then monthly appointments. During the following six months, I gave the cancer much less thought than you would expect. I never felt sick or had any discomfort. As big of a bombshell as the "you have cancer" statement had been when I originally got the news, I basically forgot about it (or ignored it), unless a family member or close friend brought it up while touching base. That was true until the doctor's office called in month seven. It was now November 2015, and for me to continue as a patient, they required that I come in and sign a waiver clarifying that we understood the doctor's diagnosis and were refusing treatment options. This understandably unnerved Victoria and, faced with this option, we met with the doctor and agreed to do an updated, repeat comprehensive biopsy to track the cancer's growth. I was not thrilled, as it is a painful procedure, but I understood the rationale. While it's not generally advisable to do a repeat biopsy within twelve months, at this point we were well off the standard chart of recommendations and I admit that I was a bit curious myself. Not worried, but curious.

The doctor called with the biopsy results a few days later. As I was in the car and on my way to a Christian men's retreat for spiritual growth and rejuvenation, I conferenced Victoria in on the call. The doctor said, "Mark, I've got the results back, and it's not what I expected. There is no trace of cancer. None. You're cancer-free. I can't explain it."

Of course, *I* could explain it. God had kept His promise. Victoria and I shared tears of happiness and talked about what that meant for our future, and then I continued on my way to the retreat. When I arrived, I greeted my friend Jim, the organization's founder, and told him about my cancer miracle. He asked if I would give a word to the attendees in the morning before the keynote speaker, and I agreed. After all, that was the deal I made with God, right? He had done His part; now, it was time for me to testify to His grace in Christ.

A friend introduced me, saying, "Mark Negley has a word for us to get us started this morning." The men in the room were still bustling around, getting to their seats, and grabbing bacon off the breakfast bar.

I walked up to the microphone and said, "Yes, I do have a word to share this morning. That word … is *cancer*." The room, filled with a couple hundred men, got a little quieter. I leaned into the mic and said again, "Cancer." The guys stopped walking around. A third time, in the biggest, deepest voice I could muster, I said, "Cancer." I had everyone's attention.

I proceeded to tell the group the whole story about my cancer journey, including, of course, God waking me up at 4:00 in the morning with a promise. At the end, I said, "I'm not a faith healer. I don't have any answers. I'm just the recipient of God's grace and someone in need of His love, just like you guys. But I have a feeling there's someone here today who's in a similar situation. I didn't tell many people that I had cancer during the last six months. I bet I'm not the only one who keeps that kind of news to himself. That's what we do, right? We isolate. We keep these things to ourselves, relying on our own strength and power. We try to muscle through it on our own. But that's not a good response. If you're quietly struggling this morning, I encourage you to talk to someone. God healed me because He wants me to share His grace and power with you. If there's anyone who'd like to pray with me, just let me know."

About ten seconds later, a friend of mine, Tom, stood up in the middle of the room. He said, "I was diagnosed with prostate cancer a month ago, and I haven't told a soul."

A man at another table stood up and said, "I've been fighting lung cancer for three months. Nobody knows."

Another guy. Then another. And another.

In all, twelve men out of the two hundred stood up and revealed their struggles with cancer and other serious medical conditions. Most of them had never told anyone. That all changed that morning. Did God heal all of them like He chose to do with me? No. But He brought a new peace and comfort to them in their fight, because He reminded them that His grace, power, and love were greater than anything they were facing. And, for whatever reason, He chose to do it through me.

In the coming months, I continued to share my story of God's grace and healing. I was given the opportunity to speak at a couple of men's groups and retreats and in the various small groups we attended. I felt I was starting to fulfill my end of the blessing and commission I had received from God, but I had the notion that there must be more to the story. My testimony was simple enough: that when facing adversity—no matter how stressful and uncertain—His grace was enough to bear all things, that a relationship with God could and *did* make a huge difference. And, for whatever reason, He had chosen to heal me. God had brought me through some incredible trials that had tested my faith, and He had called me to share that journey with others. What could be better?

After everything my family had experienced, I figured that maybe now we'd been through the worst.

I couldn't have been more wrong.

Into the Valley

The next spring, we were looking forward to celebrating a monumental achievement: our son's high school graduation. He had overcome so much to get to this point, battling significant learning differences that would have broken many kids. We were so proud of him. On top of it all, he was an accomplished high school athlete with four collegiate scholarship offers for cross-country. Against the odds, he had made it through high school and was about to attend college—on scholarship, no less! We had many people to thank for their support, patience, and friendship, not the least of who were the headmasters of the middle and high schools who had bet on Andersen to succeed and accepted him when most others would not. With his graduation approaching in May 2016, Victoria and I really wanted to celebrate his accomplishments.

We started planning a graduation party two months before gradua-tion, inviting friends and family from all over the country to join us in the Buffalo area to celebrate and encourage Andersen. As is a tradition for the male graduates in our family, we were planning his "Manhood Tribute" dinner event where family members were asked to provide encourage-ment, insights, and fun stories. Victoria had been on a carefully concocted mix of antidepressants we had collaborated on and tested with doctors over the past four years. The medications were working, and the past two years had been mostly uneventful and positive. However, the medications had one clear side effect: weight gain. I knew this was an issue for her and I understood it, but it was a non-issue for me. I thought she looked great, and the flip side of the coin was far more frightening and a powerful deterrent to messing with medication dosage.

After a week of hearing her plans to lose fifteen pounds before graduation and just one day after sending out graduation party invites, she jumped into bed without touching her bedside meds. On an unofficial watch, I asked if she was going to take her medication. "Already did," she said, and that was that. The next night I went upstairs to read well before Victoria, knowing her typical evening dosage had not been touched. This time, with the lights already out, she jumped into bed without a pause. This time I made it an issue. Turning the lights on I told her I knew she had not taken her medication and I was not comfortable with this strategy. Defiant, she laid it out for me, "I feel fine, and I want to lose fifteen pounds. I can't do that on these pills so I'm going to cut back on my medicine." When I protested, Victoria made it was clear I was not in charge of her or this decision and this was the way it was going to be. "Don't worry," she said, trying to reassure me, "everything is going to be fine." Her mind was made up, but I was apprehensive.

I had learned that this is a very common challenge for families going through the heartbreaking struggle with depression and mental health challenges. Victims oftentimes struggle with the paradoxical relationship of feeling better on medication to the point they feel they no longer need them. Once off meds, their symptoms return and it can be a vicious cycle. For those of you, like me, who have been through it, I'm sure you can appreciate that this is why mental health disease is considered a family disease. We will also explore this issue more deeply in a later chapter about living with ongoing hardships.

As the next four weeks passed, I could see the toll the chemical shift was taking on my wife. By the time graduation weekend arrived, any hint of celebration was lost behind Victoria's dark eyes and forced smile. She was struggling. Even at the big party following graduation, I could tell she was fighting to put on a happy face. Others noticed too. Friends and family members pulled me aside and asked about her. I did my best to reassure them, while also trying to manage Victoria's mental health struggles *and* give my son the attention he deserved at that milestone celebration. Looking back, that entire weekend looks like a house of cards fighting to stand in the face of a stiff wind.

With the graduation and party behind us, it was a relief to get home on Monday without incident. After a long night's sleep, things seemed to change dramatically for the better. Victoria was a completely different person. Her demeanor was light and airy, and she seemed happy—*truly* happy, and not the forced happy she'd attempted to display all weekend. I assumed she'd gone back on her medicine, but that was a sensitive topic for her, so I didn't directly address it. She, Andersen, and I spent Tuesday afternoon in my home office looking over his athletic scholarship offers and deciding which school was the best fit and which offered the necessary academic support. It was a good day for our family. I thought, *Maybe now things can get back to normal for all of us.*

But things would never be normal again.

The next day, I worked, ran some errands, and then hit a few golf balls in the afternoon. I called Victoria on my way home, but I couldn't reach her. After a few failed attempts, I called Andersen. He was home playing video games and reported that his mother wasn't there. From his view, she was gone when he returned home from his afternoon training run.

About a mile from home, I felt a panic sweeping over me. I couldn't explain it. I had to get home. *I had to find my wife.*

I hit my street and raced toward the house. I swung into the driveway and jammed my thumb into the button on the garage door opener. As the door rose, I saw Victoria's car parked right there where it was supposed to be. There was an audible sigh of relief as I inched my car into the adjacent garage bay, but something just did not seem right. That light sigh turned into a gasp of horror when I pulled in just a bit more. There, just on the other side of Victoria's Land Rover, hung her now-lifeless body.

Victoria had taken her life.

Shock. Complete and utter shock.

Forgetting to even put the car in park, I jumped out in a primal panic. I jumped back in and threw the car into park. I didn't know what to do. *Dear God, what do I do?!*

I cried out in anguish as I embraced Victoria's lifeless body trying not to panic more and struggling to comprehend the situation and come up with a plan of action. Andersen heard my cries from inside and burst through the door leading from the house into the garage. He could barely understand the scene in front of him. Seeing him dumbstruck and reeling backwards into the wall brought me to my senses. I gently released my hold on Victoria's body, rushed over to the door, pushed Andersen back inside the house, and told him to call 911.

It was all a blur. While holding her body, I grabbed a knife and cut the ski rope, gently placing her body on the garage floor. The sight and experience were far more than I could bear. Thankfully, a nearby neighbor who works as a paramedic heard the 911 call on her monitoring channel, rushed through the open garage door, and softly pushed me aside so she could attend to Victoria's body. I stumbled back against the wall and tried to stand up. I couldn't. Additional paramedics and police officers raced in just behind my neighbor. One officer approached me with compassion as I crawled over toward him on the garage floor like a lost and wounded animal. He kindly offered me a hand, lifted me up, and helped me into the house. I was losing it.

I pulled myself together enough to call my pastor, Cliffe, who raced over and was there in less than ten minutes following my panicked voice message. I then called my brother and sister, struggling to tell them what was happening and scarcely able to believe the words coming out of my mouth. Over the next hour, Andersen sat dumbfounded on the sofa while we talked to a million different people. I questioned my pastor about the heaven-and-hell consequences of suicide that my childhood religion had somehow ingrained in my mind. Detectives scoured our home looking for a suicide note and, I'm sure, signs of foul play. I was gently interrogated and the police questioned my son separately. Paramedics came and went. Organ donor people called and kept me on the phone for a half hour. Every moment, every conversation, every realization led me deeper and deeper into this nightmare.

Hours passed. Finally, around 1:00 a.m., the last person left, and Andersen and I stood in the kitchen alone.

There were no words.

Questions for Discussion

1. Describe the first time you ever felt genuine loss and heartache. Examples might include the death of a precious childhood pet, the loss of a parent at a young age, a broken relationship, your parents' divorce, learning disabilities, medical challenges, and so forth. In what ways did that loss change your life?

2. If your journey includes a battle with mental or emotional health issues (yours or a loved one's), describe the unique challenges you faced coming to terms with it. What was your reaction? How did others react? What social stigmas did you face?

3. If your journey includes a battle against a frightening medical diagnosis (yours or a loved one's), describe the situation and explain how you felt the moment you got the news. Did you share it with anyone, or were you more inclined to keep it to yourself?

4. My cancer story ended with a miraculous healing and faith experience. What is your reaction to that story? Does your faith/worldview allow for such seemingly unexplainable phenomena?

5. Sometimes, it seems the challenges of life pile up one on top of another. Just as we get hit on one side, we're already bracing for a hit on the other. Have life's hits piled up on you? How so?

6. How do you think you would have reacted if you had experienced a similar moment of finding your spouse or another family member the way I did? What emotions and thoughts might have run through your mind during such an unbelievably painful experience?

Chapter 3

SURVIVAL MODE

*T*HE BEST WAY I CAN DESCRIBE THE DAYS IMMEDIATELY FOLLOWING the death of my wife is *survival mode*. Sometimes, the absolute best we can do is to simply *survive* the tragedy playing out in front of us. My hope is that, in reading my story, you realize you're not alone when you experience the pain of losing someone you love or another life tragedy.

The morning after Victoria's death, I stumbled into the kitchen completely shell-shocked. It was 7:00 a.m. on a Thursday morning. My mind was on overload, my heart was aching, and my body was numb. The waves of grief had ebbed and flowed through the restless night. I had cried on and off until around 4:00 a.m. when I finally passed out from sheer exhaustion. Now, almost in a trance, I rummaged through the fridge for something to eat and made a pot of coffee. I ventured upstairs to my office and saw Andersen's scholarship materials lying where we had left them on Tuesday afternoon and thought, *Was that really just the day before yesterday?* So much had changed since then, and the college choices and related priorities that felt so urgent and important less than thirty-six hours earlier didn't seem to matter anymore.

I couldn't wrap my head around what all had happened. I felt guilt for missing what must have been obvious warning signs. Did Victoria try to tell me what was about to happen, and did I ignore her? I tried to fight off an onslaught of self-doubt and attacks by the enemy. Had I failed my wife as her husband? What could I have done differently? I was eaten up inside with the question of what I *could* have done . . . *should* have done . . . to prevent this tragedy. Those questions ate at me for a long time, but those first few days were the hardest.

I am grateful to be close with my siblings, both of whom came to help as soon as I told them of Victoria's death. My brother, as a gung-ho former West Point graduate and Ranger, had hung up from our call, grabbed his toiletries, and jumped in his car. His plan was *action*—to come to his brother's aid immediately, driving directly to Connecticut from Nashville through the night. My sister, a doctor who was on a family vacation, booked the first available flight from Florida and arrived at LGA at 10:00 a.m. Despite the circumstances, we laughed that she had beaten our brother who had stopped, exhausted, at a hotel in the early morning hours. We were all together by Thursday afternoon, the day after Victoria's death. I will never forget their acts of kindness and support in my time of need.

The shock of the event was compounded by physical exhaustion. For days, I couldn't eat a full meal or sleep more than a couple hours at a time. No matter what time I went to bed, my eyes seemed to open at 3:19 a.m., leaving me tired and ill-equipped for the decisions I'd have to make, the conversations I'd have to have, and the actions I'd have to take that day. It became obvious why survivors are so often prescribed sedatives in the days after a loss. It's the only way many of us can get any rest in our shell-shocked, overloaded, survival-mode state. Otherwise, we're just living on adrenaline, grief, and faith. I chose to push my way through without medication, preferring to be as present as possible (although tired) and deal with whatever was required. I felt I needed to be there for Andersen. It was the right choice for me, though I certainly realize this is a personal decision and everyone needs to do what is right for them.

In the Park at 3:32 A.M.

Friday morning, my eyes opened—wide awake—again at 3:19 a.m. The same thing happened the next day. And the next. And the next. It was the strangest thing. On that first morning, after tossing, turning, and fighting flashbacks from the previous day's events, the clock turned to 3:32 a.m. and I decided to get up and go for a walk—something I continued to do each morning afterward. It was the same odd routine. After initially waking, wrestling with the moment, and trying to get a bit more sleep, I would roll over and look at the clock. When it hit 3:32, I'd give up and head to Irwin Park. Still dark and quiet, I found comfort and peace on these early morning walks with God. He and I got a lot of work done while the rest of the world slept.

In my experience, it's in times of loss and brokenness that the rubber meets the road for a person of faith. These are the moments and seasons of our lives when we have the opportunity and choice to make an intentional decision to lean in closer to God and hold on more tightly than at any other time in our journey.

For many people I've talked to about this, they grew up believing that God loves them and would always be there for them—that he might even protect them from all harm. It can come as quite a surprise, then, when bad things happen. Regardless of your theological understanding, it's normal to want to know how and why a loving God could let this happen. Did He *cause* it or did He merely *allow* it? Why? Did He not care enough about me to prevent it? Is it enough to know that He's standing by your side in the aftermath? How does He expect you to react? How will this shocking loss affect your faith?

For those of us thrust into the unique situation of suicide, we can also struggle with unfounded and misguided religious doctrine that suggests someone taking their own life prevents them from going to heaven. I know I did. In fact, as I mentioned, that was the first question I asked my pastor when he walked into my home that evening, mere minutes after Victoria's death. I was blessed to receive a compelling answer to this question, as there are Scripture passages that are crystal clear about God's love and how suicide does not limit His love, grace, forgiveness, and acceptance. In fact, nothing can or does limit His love. For example, I found—and still find—great comfort in Paul's letter to his church plant in Rome when he wrote, "I am convinced that neither death nor life, neither angels nor demons, neither the present nor the future, nor any powers, neither height nor depth, nor anything else in all creation will be able to separate us from the love of God that is in Jesus Christ our Lord" (Romans 8:38–39). For me, it brought great comfort to know that Victoria was safely in His loving arms, regardless of how she had returned home to him.

That said, there are a lot of faith-related questions we are compelled to ask when we lose someone we love. In my case, I asked God a catalog's worth of them on our predawn walks. My understanding was that the world and its brokenness are a predictable end result of God granting us the ability to live a life of freedom and choice, and my questions were in the context of that faith-driven worldview. It did not occur to me to be angry with Him, as I do not believe He causes bad things to happen in the world. In fact, He was the one resource in this time that I knew I could count on for grace and support while the world was failing me. He was where I could turn to for answers, insights, support, and comfort. I needed Him more than ever.

Since no one else was at the park at 3:32 a.m., I asked Him my questions out loud. My preference has always been to engage God verbally, passionately, and personally. So there we were, every morning . . . walking and talking. I would ask my questions, and He would answer. Not audibly—that's only happened once in my life—but I felt His responses in my spirit, which brought me needed comfort in spite of the pain and suffering I was experiencing. I believe this is what the Apostle Paul meant when he described being given the gift of "the peace of God, which transcends all understanding" (Philippians 4:7).

It was during these times that I depended most heavily on my relationship with Jesus Christ. He assured me that He was with me, that He loved

Victoria, that she was safe with Him, and that I could trust Him. When I wasn't sure of anything else, God wouldn't let me forget that He was my friend. Talking with God gave me the sense and comfort that He knew the answers and would reveal them in time. While I did not get direct answers to all my questions, He was present, patient, and loved me no matter the grief I was experiencing. He wasn't a cosmic puppeteer pulling all the strings; He was my Lord and a friend who understood what I was going through and had promised to walk through it with me.

His grace inspired me to try to walk in a way that would honor my wife's memory. I don't believe that I could have made it through without His presence.

Music and Grieving

I cannot overstate the importance of music to me at this time in my journey. As I listened to music and grieved with songs, I found that they comforted my heart, soothed my soul, and inspired strength. For me, songs of worship were critical in the dark of night, alone in my bed and grieving. Some were familiar songs that suddenly had a meaning much more pointed and powerful in this new context. Some were new songs that fit my situation in ways that felt like they were written for me and for this moment. And others were favorites I had shared with my wife that were reminders of happier days together.

Often, I would put a certain selection on repeat, lie in bed, and listen to it over and over until the warm blanket of sleep would cover me. Awakening to the same song was somehow comforting. I developed playlists that were intended to serve a specific purpose, and I found myself at times *needing* to listen to a specific song. I wore out several worship songs with which I felt a deep connection and listened to pop, rock, and country music that Victoria and I had enjoyed together. Songs that were directly connected to memories we had shared together were connective and cathartic, although early in the survival experience, they were frequently too emotional to listen to for long. It was important to be intentional about my choices. Music was a constant companion, essential to my grieving process. For examples of my favorite songs and those from others who have been inspired by music in their grief journey, you can visit www.SurviveAliveThrive.org and click on the "Resources" tab. While there, you can connect with others in our online grief community and also share your own playlist suggestions to inspire others while you browse.

Their Mere Presence a Comfort

At this early stage following a traumatic loss, a surviving spouse or parent is often thrust into a million different conversations—most of which I sincerely did not want to have. In my situation, the phone calls, texts, and doorbells started immediately. Fortunately, my sister, Carolyn, became the gatekeeper; I gave her my phone and she took charge of the front door, and every visitor and caller had to go through her. That was the greatest gift she could have given me at the time—something for which I will be forever grateful. If you are blessed to have someone you can trust to field your calls and visitors, I strongly urge you to accept their offer of grace as I did.

In the immediate aftermath of a traumatic event, many people you're close to will struggle to know how they can provide comfort and support. I have experienced this myself and have heard stories of well-intended friends and family who unintentionally brought more pain and stress while trying to help.

"What can I do for you?" is a common question, which inadvertently puts the pressure back on you to come up with ways or tasks for helping. "Are you okay?" is another question people ask—when you are clearly *not* okay. "What happened?" or "Do you want to talk about it?" are questions that can lead people directly back to their source of pain. For those who generously want to come to the aid of someone they love in this type of situation, my advice is simple: merely *being there* is the greatest gift you can provide. Stay in the moment. Let the person know you are present to comfort. Be proactive in offering specific ways you can help. That is a huge gift in and of itself. That said, be prepared for an onslaught of emotions and be willing to grieve with your friend or family member when those emotions present themselves.

On the second day after my brother arrived in Connecticut, I had one of those moments. I had just enough emotional energy to deal with the day's priorities: coordinating the timing of the memorial service and informing many of our closest friends and relatives of Victoria's death— many of whom required comforting themselves. After that, I needed recharging and alone time to continue processing my own grief. That morning, my brother, John, came into my room where I was curled up in bed, listening to music and gently weeping. He simply climbed on the bed, took my hand, and wept beside me. It was one of the most giving gestures of love I could imagine. No words were spoken; we simply cried together and rested in the truth that God's love and comfort would blanket us in that moment. That moment impacted us both deeply, and even today, we still laugh and say, "You haven't experienced sibling bonding until you've held your brother's hand and wept together in bed!" For me, it was a heart-felt statement, and I am deeply grateful he had the insight and compassion not to speak but to be merely present.

Dealing with Friends and Family

Being part of such a close family and concerned community is obviously a comfort, but it could also be a source of unintended pain. The cavalcade of family members, friends, neighbors, pastors, church members, and busi-ness associates forced me to relive the tragedy several times a day. Every time someone asked me how I was, I had to go back to the well of my pain to draw out an answer. Every "I'm so sorry" threw the reality of my loss back in my face. I'm sure that's why so many people adopt a stoic, almost-robotic "I'm fine" response as a defense mechanism. Anything more than a curt "fine" can send us back into the grief spiral. We will talk more about coping and communication strategies in section 2.

It may seem harsh to say we're *required* to deal with loving and concerned family members, friends, and service providers, as they are there to love and support you. But it can be a fine line and an intense paradigm. It is even more complicated with family members, distant relatives, and close friends who feel they are owed a full explanation. In my case, Victoria's siblings were in disbelief that their sister would take her own life. They frequently depended on her counsel and support, and this was a shock. Even in her deepest struggles, she found comfort and distraction from her own problems by focusing on how to help *them*.

Questions were generally posed carefully and gently, but it was clear that some questions were an interrogation on what had *really* happened. The bottom line is that some people with whom you thought you had close relationships can ask questions or make statements that cause you to feel blamed or criticized. Be prepared to deal with this issue and know you are not alone, as this is not an uncommon occurrence among the people I have interviewed and talked with about loss.

Things get even trickier for those with whom you have unresolved conflict, especially if there's longstanding animosity or estrangement in the relationship. In our case, Victoria and I had a significant disagreement with one of her brothers and his girlfriend a couple of weeks before her death. The disagreement and hard feelings had festered, and we had not had the chance to reconcile those differences. And now a sister he dearly loved was gone. He was in pain, and I understood that.

My brother, after hearing about the situation, encouraged me to go meet with them to try and bring healing, understanding, and comfort.

With his support and companionship, I went on behalf of my wife, and I would do it again, regardless of the outcome. While I felt like it was my duty to honor Victoria and share her privately expressed desire to forgive and request forgiveness, it was also incredibly hard. In talking with others who have gone through similar situations, I found that it can be an enormous burden for someone who's struggling with their *own* trauma and brokenness to then feel obligated to make others feel better about *their* loss experience.

Of course, emotions are raw during these times. Everyone is hurting, and everyone is entitled to experience their loss. However, when you've just lost your spouse or close family member, it's fair to say that your patience for consoling others can quickly run thin. The whole situation is a powder keg, and all it takes is a spark to ignite an argument that makes the whole thing worse for everyone. I share this with you so you'll know these are common experiences for those of us who have lost loved ones. Try to have grace for others and for yourself. It's not easy, but you are not alone in this regard. Everyone is trying to get through a situation that they are struggling to understand and comprehend.

Dealing with Details

With every loss, there are several practical details that have to be sorted through. The first detail is often deciding on a communication strategy. And, of course, that includes communicating *how you want to communicate* and what level of detail is appropriate for each person. Your church wants to know what to tell people. Your family wants to know what to tell people. Your friends, your boss, your neighbors—everyone wants to know what they should tell everyone else. Again, this can be a huge stressor, particularly in the case of a suicide. My instinct was to protect Victoria by being vague and general about the facts of her death. At my direction, we initially released a formal statement that acknowledged her death, gave no cause, and asked for patience and prayers as we tried to figure out our next steps. In retrospect, this was a good strategy. It allowed me to fully articulate the message on paper, and it gave the concerned parties a script to use whenever someone asked them what happened. I eventually got more comfortable sharing the details, but that came with time and perspective. I honestly wasn't sure what to tell people in the first few days.

The next most obvious, practical detail following this kind of loss is the memorial service. This is such an odd thing, especially if you want to have the service quickly. Imagine having breakfast with your spouse one morning and sitting at a funeral home planning his or her funeral the next. If you've been through this, you know that's not an exaggeration; it literally happens that quickly.

Who will lead the service? Who will give a eulogy? What music will you play? Will there be a slideshow, and, if so, who will make it? Photos? Cremation or casket? Will there be a separate burial service? A separate family visitation service the day before? Where will these things take place? There are so many questions, and oftentimes no one else can answer them.

In my case, we had an unusual but positive situation where we had close relationships with pastors and congregants from three different churches we had attended. After sorting through availabilities, we scheduled the service at the Congregational Church of New Canaan, where we had attended when we had first become Christians. It felt like we were going home, and it felt right. I asked all three pastors to play a role in the service, and all were selfless and accommodating, genuinely focused on serving my needs and honoring the life of Victoria. The service was set, and I felt it was a blessing and God's plan that it came together as it did.

As mundane as these tasks can seem in a time of grief, they are the kind of practical details that we all have to face during the worst moments of our lives. Hopefully, if anything, they can serve as a distraction in the process of honoring someone you have loved and lost.

Greater Than That

Over the course of that first week of early morning walks, God repeatedly impressed one message on my heart. It seemed like He had the same answer for nearly every question I asked. Was I going to make it through this? Was Andersen going to be okay? Was Victoria now safe in His arms? Will our family and friends understand? I pounded Him with question after question, and His response, deep in my spirit, was always, "I'm greater than that."

Soon that became my mantra: God is greater than that. Greater than suicide. Greater than mental illness. Greater than grief. Greater than depression. Greater than death itself. Greater than what society will think. "Greater Than That" became the drumbeat by which I marched through my healing journey. In fact, it was so central to my experience that it became the guiding inspiration that compelled me to eulogize Victoria at her memorial service ten days after her death. Two close friends of ours spoke, followed by Victoria's brother Andy, and then I gave the final eulogy. From the outside, the service had an air of celebration. We had all agreed beforehand that we would meet to celebrate Victoria's life, not to focus on mourning her death. Those speaking focused on sharing stories of how she lived a life that touched others and how she loved them well.

The closing eulogy I presented reads like a transcript of a week's worth of my 3:32 a.m. walking conversations with God. Addressing our friends and family, I chose to speak honestly with them about her battle with depression and medications. I spoke directly about the fact that she committed suicide, and I urged everyone in attendance to take mental illness challenges seriously and be vigilant with their loved ones struggling with these issues. I urged all to reject any sense of guilt, shame, or embarrassment, and I shared that we had chosen not to be further victimized by any of the other life-threatening social stigmas associated with suicide and depression.

I also addressed forgiving and forgiveness, which were strong themes in Victoria's heart throughout her struggles. I spoke about what a wonderful wife and amazing mother she was, how much she loved her friends, and how caring and empathetic she was, even in her troubles. I told the crowd that, from the moment I met her, Victoria made me want to be a better man. She still does.

I shared a story of a friend who had what she described as a "God experience" after learning of Victoria's death. Karen, a friend who had moved from Connecticut to Tulsa the previous year, went to bed heartbroken the night after receiving word of Victoria's passing. She called to tell us that she had been awakened at 2:00 a.m. by what she described as the material and physical presence of the Holy Spirit—angels maybe—perhaps even Jesus Himself. She had a sensation of angels' wings fluttering close and surrounding her. It was so real, she said, that she slowly reached over to turn her bedside lamp on in hopes of seeing angels face-to-face. As the light clicked on, she found herself seemingly alone. At that moment, however, she explained she felt God clearly tell her, "She is with Me. *She is with Me.*" If you are interested in reading the full eulogy I shared at Victoria's memorial service, I have included it as an addendum at the end of this book.

In the years that have passed, I have heard many first-person stories of God's supernatural presence during the grief and brokenness people feel after losing someone they love. I have been blessed by such stories that include Victoria's niece Kimberly having visions of what she described as "her aunt's radiant, smiling, and happy face" prior to and during the memorial service, as well as that of a good friend who shared a vision he had of Victoria's kind and smiling face in the early dawn at his mother's home while he was looking at a painting of Christ on the cross that had been there since his childhood.

I was touched and deeply grateful for these and other stories that followed. It is truly amazing where the blessings come from in the midnight hour of your soul.

After the service, the family held a large luncheon to celebrate Victoria's life. The room was filled with so much laughter and joy—not what you'd expect following the memorial service of a woman who was missed by so many, but we couldn't help it. Everyone had a story to share about how Victoria lived, laughed, and loved. Our memories fueled a celebration none of us will ever forget. You may have heard the saying, "People never remember most of what you *say*, but they will always remember how you made them *feel*." Never has that been more on display than at our luncheon in Victoria's honor. It was a gathering full of people actively remembering and honoring how she made them feel.

I must acknowledge that this kind of celebration was only possible because we all knew Victoria was safe in the arms of God, as she knew Jesus and His promises personally. I knew—we *all* knew—that she was alive, renewed, healed, whole, and happy. Not since my mother's death had I been so overwhelmingly thankful for the worldview I had in Christ's love and grace. Only through that lens was I able to laugh and smile the day we gathered to celebrate a life we all loved and would miss every day from that point on.

After the memorial service, I got dozens of emails, texts, and calls from people who had heard my eulogy. Nearly everyone said something like, "Thank you for testifying to the grace of God" or, "Thanks for encouraging us with stories of God's grace." The word *grace* appeared in practically every email. As I reflected on that word—*grace*—I thought back to the covenant agreement that had been offered to me by God during my cancer ordeal. He had said, "You will be healed, and then I will reveal your commission." He had led me to Acts 20:23–24, "I consider my life worth nothing to me; my only aim is to finish the race and complete the task the Lord Jesus has given me—*the task of testifying to the good news of God's grace*" (emphasis added). Then it dawned on me: *This* was the moment God had been preparing me for. *This* was why He healed my cancer. *This* was the time to testify to God's grace.

I was overwhelmed. God wasn't just with me in my heartache; He had been preparing me for it for over a year.

When the Lasagna Stops, Go to Hawaii

It's impossible to overstate the blessing of community in the healing process. My church organized a six-week meal service for Andersen and me, with a different family preparing and delivering a meal three or four nights a week. At first, in my misguided attempt to grieve in isolation, I resisted the meals. Thankfully, my sister overrode that thought process.

I grew to look forward to those meals—despite the fact that they were *always* far too big for just my son, sister, and me, and it was *almost always* some form of pasta or other fattening, delicious dish. It wasn't just the food that I loved; it was the gesture. For someone else to think of us, sign up to prepare a meal, cook it just for us, and then deliver it to our home . . . the endless acts of love were staggering. It helped me realize I wasn't alone in this fight. Those meals and demonstrations of kindness helped meet my practical needs in a time when I couldn't have done it on my own. For that I am also deeply grateful to Grace Church and the community of New Canaan.

It was through this experience that I was reminded of an important lesson I had learned while reading Don Piper's book *90 Minutes in Heaven*. As he lay helplessly in his hospital bed following a horrific car accident, his friend and former pastor, Jay B. Perkins, had scolded him for not allowing others to help him by bringing food, books, or flowers in an attempt to ease his suffering and discomfort. The lesson he recounted was that by allowing others to help in his time of need, he was not only being blessed, but actively blessing others by allowing them to serve in the role of comforter. Piper wrote that he was "eternally grateful for the lesson of allowing people to meet my needs." I, also, am deeply grateful for gaining the same insight.[2]

The meals ended six weeks later, and the world moved on—whether my heart and soul were ready for it or not. New losses and people needed to be attended to and supported. My brother returned home the week following Victoria's service, and my sister had to return home to her job and family after generously staying an extra week to help me cope and organize. The reality was sinking in that the world was continuing to spin. I had a moment of panic. The fact that I had reached the end of the lasagna deliveries was surprisingly jarring and emotional. It's as though the love and support of others had held back the coming wave of reality, but it was now time to face it.

At this time, it was clear that Andersen and I needed to get away, to grieve and process all we'd been through somewhere other than home. Thinking of how we could do so while honoring the memory of Victoria, I decided to book a two-week trip to Maui for us. The goal was to reset, recharge, and get away from the million reminders of what we'd lost. I reminded Andersen that Hawaii was where I had met and fallen in love with his mom.

We were fortunate to have had this option. Many people are pushed back into the hard world of responsibility without nearly so much flexibility. Our trip included fun in the sun, enjoying the beautiful beaches of Maui, and time together away from it all. We walked the beaches day and night, and Andersen listened (sometimes even patiently) to his dad cry, laugh, and tell stories about our family and his mother's life. It was the healing kick-start we desperately needed.

Away from it all, we had celebrated, loved, and laughed again. But now it was time to return home and face the life decisions that awaited us. We boarded the flight a bit sunburned but rested. We weren't sure what it would be like to walk through the front door of the home we had built as a family, knowing that Victoria was gone and realizing we had to start over.

2   Don Piper, *90 Minutes in Heaven*, 2004. Chapter 9 "Endless Adjustments," page 99.

Questions for Discussion

1. Describe the morning after your loss. What was your mindset? How present were you mentally and emotionally?

2. Who did you call in the immediate aftermath of your loss? Why did you call those specific people?

3. How did your loved ones help and comfort you in the days and weeks after your loss? What act(s) of love made the most impact on you?

4. We'll see throughout this book that good people often say dumb things in the face of tragedy. How did your loved ones hurt you in the days after your loss? What did they do or say that unintentionally caused your pain?

5. I described the initial days after Victoria's death as "survival mode." Does that resonate with you? What did "survival mode" mean for you?

6. I found some degree of peace and comfort in my early morning, pre-dawn walks in the park. What helped you think more clearly in the days after your loss?

7. If you are a person of faith, how did your loss affect your relationship with God? Did you blame Him, seek comfort in Him, or something else?

8. I explained how I asked God many important questions after Victoria's death. What questions did you ask God (or want to ask God) after your loss? Did you get any answers?

9. Every loss includes a million pesky little details and responsibilities at a time when we're least able to put our full attention on them. What practical matters surprised you after your loss? How well did you handle the new demands placed on you at that time?

10. I describe how God impressed one central message on my heart in the days after Victoria's death: God is greater than that. How do you react to that statement?

Chapter 4

MOVING FORWARD

———

ANDERSEN AND I RETURNED HOME FROM HAWAII WITH MIXED emotions. We'd had a much-needed father-son escape and had been relatively protected from all the little reminders that otherwise would have forced us to relive our pain a thousand times a day. Away from our home, community, and army of well-wishers, we had been able to huddle together for two weeks to begin the healing process. It was also a wonderful time of faith-building for Andersen. Losing his mother gave him an entirely new filter through which to view life, death, and the possibility of eternal life. Matters of faith were no longer theoretical. It's one thing to wonder where we go when we die; it was quite another thing for him to discuss where *his mother* was now that she *had* died. We shared deep, loving, reflective, and sometimes painful conversations on the beach under the warm Hawaii sun, but now we were returning to the battlefield of grief.

My first indication that things would never be the same came as we turned onto our street on the way home from the airport. My hand instinctively reached for the garage door opener, and I was instantly filled with the same sense of dread I had the evening of Victoria's death, when that little button opened the door to a painful new world of loss and heartache. I chose to park in the driveway to unpack the car. The hits kept coming as we made our way into the house. Looking around our home for the first time in two weeks, I was struck by how everything I saw was filled with meaning. Victoria's presence was in every piece of furniture and décor—not to mention the dozens of family photos lovingly placed strategically throughout the house and on the walls. Items from her memorial service were front and center in the family room, including the poster-size pictures of Victoria that had been placed on easels and the photo boards with dozens of memories carefully arranged for display at the reception. There were other reminders, too, in the half-finished tasks, unpaid bills, unanswered mail, college orientation invitations, legal correspondence regarding Victoria's death and will, and pile of sympathy cards scattered across the kitchen table. Looking around at all the real-world responsibilities and being acutely aware of the inner-healing journey that awaited us, Andersen and I knew it was time to get to work. We'd been pushed around by unthinkable hardships for the past few months. Now it was time to push back.

Getting My Head on Straight

Losing someone is always traumatic, no matter the circumstances. For some of us, though, there's an extra layer of trauma when the loss is filed under "special circumstances," such as suicide. In hindsight, I wasn't just experiencing grief; I was overcome with a world of emotions, including guilt (*Was this my fault?*), confusion (*What was she thinking?*), despair (*How could she do this to us?*), abandonment (*She left me all alone just as our son leaves home for college?*), and more. I knew I had a *lot* to unpack.

Fortunately, I was connected to a wonderful counselor. George was uniquely qualified to help me start my healing journey. He had been a 9/11 first responder, so he was experienced in facing and overcoming overwhelming trauma, including seeing death up close and personally as I had. In addition to being a trauma specialist, George was also a marriage counselor, so he brought some much-needed perspective to my unresolved emotions as a newly minted widower and single father. There were so many conversations I wanted to have with Victoria, so many questions I wanted to ask. She'd always been the person I talked to when I was hurt and confused, but now she was the *reason* I was hurt and confused—and she was gone. That glaring silence was eating me up inside, so George suggested something I'd never considered: post-mortem marriage counseling. It sounds crazy, but it was exactly what I needed.

My counseling sessions with George gave me a forum to tell Victoria—out loud and with real emotion—how sorry I was for the pain she felt, how helpless I felt for not being able to help her, how confused I was that she had left Andersen and me alone, how guilty I felt for missing the clues that she was considering suicide, and how daunting a task it was to face the rest of my life without her. George would help keep the conversation going, occasionally answering, "If I were Victoria, I might say . . . ." It was truly a remarkable experience for me, but it certainly wasn't easy. George and I met once or twice a week for the first six months, followed by a few more months of biweekly check-ins. I cannot overstate how crucial that counseling was for my recovery. I treated my grief just as aggressively as one might treat a life-threatening medical condition, and I owe my new life (not to mention my sanity) to those long hours of talking, venting, and crying in George's office. If you're going through a tragic loss right now, trust the voice of experience when I say you *need* counseling. I know there are many questions and challenges in this arena, but it's critical to the healing process. We'll leave it at that for now, but we will specifically address and provide suggestions on how to approach and deal with the challenges of acquiring effective counseling in section 2.

Andersen also agreed to go to counseling during the six weeks he had at home before heading to college, but he wasn't exactly a willing participant at first. He had a very cut-and-dried, matter-of-fact perspective on his mother's death at that point. His thinking was, *Look, this is bad. It's terrible. I love Mom. I miss her, but she's gone, and there's nothing I can do about it. Let's move on.* He had an overwhelming need for normalcy, which, as I came to learn, really meant *security*. He needed to know that he was going to be okay, that his life wouldn't be destroyed by the loss of such an important and influential person. In his mind, *normal* meant staying on track and starting school on schedule. I understood that, but I also knew he needed more support than he realized. So he agreed to see his own counselor, one that specialized in teens and college students. As the weeks passed, he found peace and healing in the sessions and worked through some of his own issues under the veil of confidentiality assured through his counselor. Once he had a taste of the experience, Andersen further agreed to see a counselor for regular check-ins once he was at college. He faced those hard sessions every week like a champ, refusing to let this horrible loss ruin his life. It's a good thing he was ready to jump in and move forward with college, as we had another challenge right around the corner.

Didn't Anyone Contact You?

Andersen and I had been home from Hawaii three weeks when we ran into another mind-blowing turn in the road. We had carefully chosen a college in New Hampshire among the handful of cross-country opportunities he had received. That was actually the last thing he, Victoria, and I had discussed and decided on as a family. After weighing all the options, we chose the school that offered the best chance for Andersen to shine and grow as an athlete. Although a D-III athletic conference college, it was relatively close (three hours by car) and was in the process of revamping their track and field and cross-country teams under the leadership of a new head coach with whom we had developed a great relationship during Andersen's recruiting visit.

Now two months following his mother's death and two weeks before the athletes were set to report for pre-season training, Andersen and I arrived on campus for his student orientation only to get the shocking news that the university had changed their plans. The coach we were excited about was no longer joining the staff because the athletic director had pulled funding for the track and field program, diverting resources to build up an alternate sport program he supported. The cross-country program was still going to happen that fall, but the newly assigned coach was given the "interim" tag, as she was the women's ski team coach who had run some track as a college athlete. As expected, the incoming track and field athletes had backed out, and most of these were dual sport athletes who were the strength of the cross-country program. The bottom line was that Andersen was practically the only incoming recruited cross-country athlete still set to join the team. We were blindsided. We had picked the university because we were convinced the team would be competing for conference and D-III championships; now, the whole cross-country program looked like an afterthought. We literally watched it fall from first to worst as we stood in the admissions office—but there was nothing we could do.

This was a crushing blow at first, but Andersen made the most of it and held his own academically, while developing solid relationships with his new coach and teammates. The upside was that he had the opportunity to experience being a number two runner on the cross-country team as a true freshman, routinely finishing in the top 30 to 40 percent of all competitors in the races he ran. At season's end, and after one trying semester, we agreed he would transfer to another school that had expressed interest in his running, a D-II school in West Virginia. While he held his own academically at his new college through the support of their gifted head of the learning support program, Andersen decided to never run collegiately again. It was a real loss, but we had a much bigger race to finish victoriously.

Cleaning House

Despite the changes in his athletic program, the day I dropped Andersen off at the college three hours from our home was one of the proudest moments of my life. He had overcome tremendous obstacles to make it to college and he was handling the loss admirably. For me, though, the drive back was tough. That's when reality set in. That's when it *really* hit me that I was heading home to a big, empty house full of memories and mementos of all that I'd lost. It wasn't a haunted house by any means; these were mostly wonderful memories of my family. But Victoria was unmistakably present all throughout our home, including her personal belongings that still occupied closets, cabinets, and drawers. When I got home, I decided it was finally time to clean house.

No one ever tells you what to do with your deceased spouse's clothes after they're gone. Victoria had many beautiful, expensive pieces that filled a walk-in closet and separate wardrobe, and I had no idea how to even start going through it all. I initially asked Victoria's family, my sister, and some of her closest female friends if they wanted anything of hers, such as a dress, jacket, or piece of jewelry. I typically received one of two very distinct reactions. People either said, "Oh, yes, I would love that. I'll think of her every time I wear it" or, "Oh, goodness no. I couldn't dream of wearing anything that belonged to Victoria. It would be too painful of a reminder." It was actually very interesting, and I was careful to discuss this with George so I did not personalize the responses as somehow hurtful or disrespectful (which they clearly were not). Such is the unexpected journey.

After only giving away a fraction of her things, and after spending far too much time slowly and painfully sorting through each piece, I realized I needed professional help. No, not a new counselor. I'm talking about a professional organizer. Enter Adele. Through a friend's recommendation, I hired her to help me sort through Victoria's belongings and organize the things I needed to sell through consignment, the things I needed to donate to charity, and—most painfully—the things I really just needed to throw away. Adele was a godsend at this chore. Originally from Trinidad, she had an airy, fun personality, but was also respectful of my wife's things and understood how difficult this was for me. She was a pro in every sense of the word, and, with her help, I was able to clear out most of Victoria's belongings—except for the key pieces I chose to keep for myself. I pulled aside a few things that held special meaning for me and hid those items away in a closet and worked with Adele to let go of everything else.

Clothes weren't the only items I had to deal with, of course. Victoria had filled our home with photographs of Andersen, me, and herself. There were vacation pictures, photos from special occasions and holidays, and other perfectly framed family memories in every room. I didn't want to purge my home from all these memories, but I knew I needed to trim it down a bit. Seeing Victoria's face on every wall of every room was just too much. So I took careful inventory of each memento, kept the ones that were especially meaningful, and boxed up the rest. I wanted to cross paths with these memories in a positive way without being inundated and overpowered by them at every turn.

There is no single "right way" to go through this process, and I know how difficult it is. I remember exactly how it feels to think I'm packing my wife's life into boxes and giving her essence away piece by piece. If your loss is still fresh, don't rush this. There's no timeline other than what works for you. My only encouragement here is to not put it off too long, or you'll risk falling into a life of denial or creating a shrine of the one you've lost. Getting the help of a passionate but professional organizer was immensely beneficial to me, especially when I knew something had to go but I wasn't emotionally able to pack it up myself.

The Wolf Is Always at the Door

I find it interesting that, oftentimes when we get through a major loss or trauma, we can assume (and expect) the worst is behind us and the road ahead will be smooth. Well ... that has clearly *not* been my experience! If I had truly believed the worst was behind me after every setback, I would now be looking on a life of disappointment and disillusionment. Just as I got up from one hit, it seemed like another was coming right at me. While I hoped and prayed my trials would take a break after each setback I experienced, where would I be if that was my firm expectation following my mother's death in 2000? Then again after emerging victorious in the arduous legal battle over my son's education? Then after Victoria's life-threatening car accident? Then after developing and being healed of cancer? Then after Victoria's death? Then after . . . . See where I'm going with this?

In his 1989 song "New York Minute," Don Henley warned that "the wolf is always at the door."[3] That is, no matter who you are, where you are, or what you've been through, another hit is potentially waiting right around the corner. It's just how life works. I'm not saying it's healthy to be fearful and hide in your house while awaiting the next chip to fall. I'm just saying that reality dictates that more bad stuff may happen—even if bad stuff has *already* happened. As such, my advice is to celebrate every blessing and joy along the way, be ready for curveballs and setbacks, and embrace the journey. This does not mean you should be emotionally impenetrable and guarded so you can't be hurt. It means that our faith and worldview are *critical* to how we live and understand a life that will include loss, brokenness, and setbacks. We are all really proceeding through life with new trials and inevitable wounds ahead.

I am frequently asked how and why I am happy and love life after all I've been through. In that context, I have chosen to not be afraid of the

---

3   Don Henley, "New York Minute," *The End of the Innocence*, Warner Chappell Music, Inc. 1989.

next setback or the reality that we will *all* die at some point; rather, I am focused on how I am living until that time arrives. This is not a head-in-the-sand approach or a despondent doomsday sentiment. It celebrates the most beautiful wonders of the world and is about understanding the gift of life, the limited nature of its timeline, and finding comfort in the eternal love and promises of the Lord. If you're able to connect with God in that manner, trusting in the outcome, His promises allow us to experience the ultimate joy life has to offer. Through the filter of a loving God, the fact that life includes loss and brokenness is therefore something to understand and embrace, no matter how difficult. As they say in car racing: it's not how you handle the straightaways, it's how you navigate the turns in the road that win the race. My belief is that how we perceive the world and engage with God is what really matters, particularly in times of loss and brokenness. We will explore the opportunity to fully experience that joy in the third and final section of this book.

Reluctant Platforms

In the months following our return from Hawaii and Andersen's departure to college, God continued to give me opportunities to share the message that *God is greater than that.* I was amazed at all the different people around me who wanted to discuss that message. Once I started paying more attention to others' sense of loss, I saw it everywhere. I often thought back to that early morning encounter with God during my cancer journey, the moment when He woke me with the message, "You will be healed, and then I will reveal your commission." I knew in my spirit that I had been called to share the good news of God's grace to the brokenhearted. But how?

After returning to church and attending as a newly established "widower" following twenty years of marriage (a crazy moniker to wear, I thought), I was fortunate that many people reached out to offer support and share their stories—or to introduce me to someone they thought I could relate to and with whom I would connect. In view of the many calls and suggestions, I was smack dab in the middle of what I jokingly called "the heartbreak circuit," and I was now an honorary member!

I discovered that not only were we not alone, but over two hundred million Americans are directly impacted by loss each year. Think of it like a community network: at work and in every church, synagogue, gym, PTA, HOA, country club, and anywhere else people gather, you'll find people who are hurting. Because we're all part of several different social circles, hurting people have access to a larger network of *other* hurting people. That kind of social overlap kept my phone ringing with suggestions and connections. I got to know some nearby pastors pretty well, and I also got connected to other men and women who, like me, were openly sharing their stories of loss in an effort to bring comfort and community to others.

One such man was Paul, a guy who had lost his son to an opioid overdose in recent months. The young man had developed an addiction to pain killers, and the struggle eventually took his life. In response, Paul gave his life to educating students on the dangers of opioids. He was actively traveling to local high schools and became a frequent speaker to youth groups. Drawing inspiration from Romans 8:28, "In all things God works for the good of those who love him, who have been called according to his purpose," Paul declared, "This epidemic took my son, and my life will never be the same. But I'm going to spend the rest of my life doing whatever I can to bring some good from this heartache."

Paul and I had an instant kinship, as we both had committed to using the death of our loved ones to bring hope and change to a hurting world. It was something neither of us wanted, but a calling we couldn't ignore. Paul used to joke that he and I had "reluctant platforms." He was right.

The Next Step

In September 2016, an opportunity presented itself that would change my life direction. At that time, I was invited by my church's pastor to formally address the congregation on loss and how faith had impacted my experience. The eulogy I had presented at Victoria's service had been well received throughout the community, and many attendees had reached out to express their gratitude for inspiration and encouragement while they were struggling with their own experiences of loss and brokenness. The concept was that I would share a brief bit of my story during the main service and invite those struggling with loss, brokenness, and/or mental health challenges to join me, our community pastor Stuart, and a Christian-based local psychologist named Frank to discuss related issues and field questions after the service. Stu would bring the pastoral and counseling perspective, Frank would bring the clinical perspective, and I would simply share my story and represent those whose lives have been personally affected by mental health issues, children with disabilities, health crises, suicide, and other encounters with loss. We reserved a classroom to seat thirty or so people and had bagels and coffee for those who wanted to join us. We rushed down there after the service, set out our table, chairs, and bagels, and waited for the crowd.

Fifteen minutes after the end of the worship service, though, no one had shown up. As the three of us sat there, I turned to Stu and Frank and cracked, "Well, I hope you guys are hungry, because we're going to have a lot of leftover bagels." We laughed and started chatting amongst ourselves, unsure of when to call it a bust and leave. That's when the first couple nervously walked into the classroom. We greeted them as a few more walked in. Then more. And more. And more. Each person seemed genuinely surprised to find others who were interested in the discussion.

Amazingly, close to a hundred people showed up and we had to relocate to a larger conference area to handle the turnout. We each made opening statements, and then we opened the floor for questions. People shared the challenges they were facing in their marriage, their feelings of grief after losing someone, how hard it was to raise their kids, workplace stress, financial insecurity, anxiety, depression, health crises, and more. It was like we'd opened a fire hydrant, and the pressure exploded out of every person in the room. After an hour and a half of questions and discussion, we finally had to cut it off and end the meeting. Two weeks later, we hosted another session and, again, had an overwhelming turnout. It was clear we were addressing a deeply felt need to connect, share, and learn about our experiences of loss and brokenness. Often when people are experiencing loss, their pain can make them think they're all alone in their suffering; gathering together shows them that they're not. This realization can galvanize the healing process.

We were amazed and excited at what we were experiencing. These gatherings far exceeded anything we could have imagined. In retrospect, the biggest thing we were doing was giving people a safe place to voice their fears and struggles. We made it socially acceptable to be broken and, with the stigma stripped away, people felt free to be real. It's no exaggeration to say that a hundred different healing journeys began that day. I was overjoyed to see how God used our little meeting, and I couldn't wait to see what more He had in store. We found such joy in providing love to others in the midst of their stories of brokenness, but there were some challenges. Having a hundred people in one room was too much. No matter how much time we allotted, there was no way everyone could have a chance to speak. There was also no way everyone in the group could really get to know each other—an element of community we believed was extremely important to each person's healing journey. So as we held the big meetings, I got to work on something more intimate and more manageable.

Friends of Victoria

While reading the book *Anatomy of the Soul* by Dr. Curt Thompson, I was inspired by his reference to psychologist Dr. Dan Siegel's work related to personal neurobiology and his studies on measuring healing through the act of sharing life experiences with an empathetic audience.[4] He believed it was possible to measure emotional healing activity through the mere act of sharing in a safe setting. That scientifically reinforced what caring community support is all about. Excited and motivated, the next step was putting the theory into action.

Taking Siegel and Thompson's research into account and with a cue from other proven recovery and group support programs, I set out to create an environment for small group sharing specifically for people experiencing heartache and loss. It was clear that true healing could not occur as dynamically in large groups but, would happen more frequently in small communities that met regularly, fostered relationships, and created a safe place in which stigmas were expelled and each participant was fully embraced. In our case, I called the group "Friends of Victoria" (FOV)— not because everyone in the group personally knew my wife, but as a way to show we're *all* connected through our pain. The two things we communicated at every meeting and wanted everyone present to know were that (1) they were not alone because they had both a *God* and a *community* who loved them, and (2) they were in a safe, judgment-free zone where their story was important and their struggles were legitimate.

In November 2016, I was again asked to speak at the Christian men's regional retreat in Massachusetts, a year after sharing my story of healing from cancer with the same group. It was crazy timing as my beloved Cubs had just won their first World Series title in 108 years, and I had attended the Michigan Avenue parade the day before,

---

4   Curt Thompson, *Anatomy of the Soul: Surprising Connections between Neuroscience and Spiritual Practices That Can Transform Your Life and Relationships* (Tyndale Momentum, 2010).

delaying my arrival at the retreat until after 1:00 that morning. The retreat theme was on wholeness, and my talk was about relying on God along the journey, no matter what life throws your way. It was in striking contrast to the talk I had given a year earlier in which I celebrated God's grace and my being healed of cancer. Here we were a year later, and I was telling a new story: that my wife had tragically died and that God was leading me to bring comfort and hope to people who were also experiencing loss and brokenness. It was a great reminder that the road of life is unpredictable and the eternal dependability and love of God are the things we can count on. *No matter what.*

I led weekly FOV meetings for the next two years, giving up that role when I relocated to the Nashville area in 2018. During that time, I developed many wonderful friendships and was honored to walk with dozens of hurting men and women who were facing incredible loss and hardships. Some had been through the healing process and simply wanted to give back and help others on their journey. As I met more and more people and heard their incredible stories of loss and their journeys of restoration, it occurred to me that the issue of brokenness was so much bigger than any one of us. Sure, I have been through a lot personally, but so have many, many other people—men and women who have overcome more than I ever thought possible. I have been so blessed by their stories, and I knew others would be as well.

A New Model

During this period, I had the privilege to meet and brainstorm with pastors, counselors, and emotional and mental health professionals serving in the areas of faith, grief, loss, recovery, and psychology. Through these discussions and research, it has become clear to me that, although everyone has a unique story, we are all connected through the shared experience of pain. It's also evident that one of the most important steps in the healing journey is connecting with others who understand what you're going through—and that the world is *filled* with these people.

I studied the grief recovery experience, focusing on loss and healing in general terms and looking at surviving traumatic life events, and more specifically suicide. I made it a point to attend a variety of grief workshops in my quest to better understand what I was going through, how others were approaching their healing, and what to expect moving forward. However, the more I studied, the more dissatisfied I became with what I was seeing. None of them seemed to resonate with me. It seemed that most methods simply proposed going through their model in a linear fashion and achieving "healing" at the end of the process. That did not seem realistic to me on many levels and was not consistent with what I was hearing, seeing, and experiencing in the FOV meetings I hosted and in other grief groups I had attended.

At that time, a trusted mentor suggested I expand the extent of my focus and study, so I began the process of conducting formal interviews with those who had a compelling story they were willing to share. I started with FOV members and connections I had made through "the heartbreak circuit" and then began to intentionally seek out others with a story to share.

Several years later, I've now met with hundreds of people, formally interviewing dozens. My goal was to get to the heart, progression, and trajectory of the healing journey and help others better understand their experiences with loss and brokenness and find a path to happiness and ultimately joy. The stories I've had the privilege to gather are from people of different races and socio-economic backgrounds and include experiences of loss and brokenness from wives, husbands, parents, children, friends, siblings, and more. While anecdotes from some of these stories are included in this book, you can also find a variety of first-person stories and insights at the website and share your own personal story there to inspire and/or connect with others.

The new model introduced in the next section is called Survive-Alive-Thrive™ and was created to help those who have been through or are currently going through loss and brokenness to better navigate the journey from loss to hope to happiness. The model is designed to reduce stress and anxiety related to the recovery process by better understanding what we are experiencing and where we're going on the journey.

The insights generated are from people like you and me, who have lived or are currently going through their own struggles. My hope is that the process and stories shared will help you on your healing journey or to help someone you love as they do the same. We'll unpack it in the following section together.

Questions for Discussion

1. I described flashback-like feelings as I approached my garage after returning home from Hawaii with Andersen. Is there a specific place or activity that is especially painful for you in the wake of your loss? Explain.

2. What were some of the raw emotions—such as guilt, confusion, anger, abandonment, shame, and so forth—that you felt in the aftermath of your loss? Were you surprised by anything you felt?

3. Did you explore counseling after your loss? If so, describe your experience. If not, explain why you chose not to do so.

4. I share how Andersen and I were surprised and frustrated by a mix-up at his college while we were trying to "get back to normal." What new challenges, losses, or frustrations have you encountered as you've tried to reengage your life? How have you responded to them?

5. If you've lost a spouse, parent, or child, describe your experience going through your loved one's things after their death. What surprised you about the experience?

6. What does it mean to you to know that "the wolf is always at the door"? How have you already experienced this?

7. Has your loss given you a new, unexpected, or reluctant platform? Explain.

8. Have you been surprised by others' willingness to share their stories of loss with you in the wake of your own loss? How has this new community of hurting people shaped your loss experience?

9. Have you explored other avenues of grief recovery before reading this book? Examples might include other books, grief groups, and online communities. If so, describe how they've helped and share any shortcomings you've noticed as you've tried to piece your life back together.

SECTION

2

NAVIGATING THE JOURNEY

Chapter 5

UNDERSTANDING OUR HEALING JOURNEY

*I*N THE FOUR AND A HALF YEARS THAT HAVE PASSED FOLLOWING THE death of my wife, I've spoken with hundreds of people and formally interviewed dozens in various stages of their loss and healing journey. For two of those years, I've had the privilege of facilitating and participating in support groups focused on helping others through loss, grief, and recovery. While my goal has been to share lessons learned and insights gained along the way, the time and effort invested has also been a blessing and instrumental in my personal growth and pursuit of joy. Ultimately, it is my hope and prayer that these insights will help you better understand your journey and chart your own path to hope and happiness.

In my own journey, I have gained an intimate understanding of how many of us experience loss and brokenness. Among the lessons learned is that everyone—and everyone's response to loss—is *unique*. A big part of that is because we each have a specific, very special blend of personality traits, temperaments, methods of processing, emotional health status, and physiological responses to stress. In addition, our responses are influenced by faith perspectives that shape our understanding of the world, as well as our individual "backstories," which are the lessons and life experiences that shape how we see ourselves and others. Each of these variables and how they are combined contribute to how we perceive and respond to loss and to our capacity for healing.

At the same time, I've seen tremendous similarities across many different types of loss and grief experiences. It's interesting that we can have our own unique and personal experiences yet still have an amazing ability to connect and relate to one another simply through having been through loss. The fact is that none of us is immune to grief and hardship and we *all* know how it feels to face loss on some level. What's surprised me, however, is how people who have had different types of loss experiences can be deeply drawn together through their personal *response* to the grief experience more so than the *type* of loss they have experienced. You might expect that someone who's lost a young child, for example, would primarily connect and relate to another parent who's been through the same thing. But that's not always the case. Because our responses to grief can be similar across different types of loss, a mourning parent may feel more connected to or understood by someone whose *response* to the loss of a sibling or friend is more similar to theirs than to someone who's lost a child of their own but responded in a different way.

This isn't only about those grieving someone's death, however. As we'll discuss throughout this book, loss comes in many forms. People going through divorce, raising a special needs child, supporting a loved one with emotional or mental health issues, facing a frightening medical diagnosis, or struggling with financial or career issues are all experiencing a type of loss. The silver lining, though, is that this creates an enormous pool of resources we can lean on. And again, it's not just about connecting one person going through a divorce to another person going through divorce or one cancer patient to another. It's about finding other individuals or, better yet, a whole community of people who are going through a form of loss while experiencing similar emotional responses. We connect to others through *how* they experience loss much more than we do through *what* loss they're experiencing. This is an important dynamic that is lost in most traditional forms of grief/loss recovery.

The most well-known psychology-based model in the grief-recovery world is the Kübler-Ross "Five Stages of Grief." This model, introduced in the 1969 book *On Death and Dying* by noted Swiss-American psychiatrist Dr. Elisabeth Kübler-Ross, presents a concept that is linear in nature, as the survivor progresses through: (1) denial, (2) anger, (3) bargaining, (4) depression, and (5) acceptance. Linear progression models like this represent the healing experience as a series of emotional response steps that we will go through when confronted with loss. The model essentially suggests you will *first* feel this, and *then* you will feel this, and *finally* you'll feel this. As you progress, you will process the emotions associated with that step, get past them, and address the next until you have successfully completed the progression and are healed. The problem is, neither I nor any of the people I have interviewed or talked to have found the process to work like that.

When I was first introduced to the five stages of grief in my personal grief-recovery process, I learned that this model is filled with caveats. Simply put, most current psychology theory acknowledges that it doesn't work the same way for most (if any) people. In fact, contrary to popular belief, the five stages weren't even developed for people going through the grieving process; they were developed for people who were terminally ill as a way to come to terms with their impending death. It was only later retrofitted and applied to others who were left in the wake of a loved one's death.[5]

5   David B. Feldman, Ph.D., "Why the Five Stages of Grief Are Wrong: Lessons from the (non-)stages of grief," *Psychology Today*, July 7, 2017, https://www.psychologytoday. com/us/blog/supersurvivors/201707/why-the-five-stages-grief-are-wrong and Michael Shermer, "Five Fallacies of Grief: Debunking Psychological Stages," *Scientific American*, Nov 1, 2008, https://www.scientificamerican.com/article/five-fallacies-of-grief/.

In the fifty years since its introduction, there have been many itera-tions and enhancements of the five-stages model in an attempt to better illustrate the more free-flowing nature of the grief response. It's become understood that the model's stages may go in a different order and/or that one or more stages may not apply to you at all. Regardless, I couldn't help but wonder how such a grief model could be considered a universal standard yet still acknowledge the need for so many caveats, tweaks, and exceptions, particularly when applied to the death of a loved one.

On a personal level, I was also sensitive to the potential feelings I'd have if I reexperienced an emotional response tied to a "completed" earlier stage in this model of the healing process. That would feel like a regres-sion in my progress. How could a linear model work if even one of my linear-defined grief responses was potentially a long-term part of my life moving forward? In the pursuit of checking off a stage-to-stage checklist on the path to healing, that could feel like a *Groundhog Day* nightmare from which I could not escape. The risk of adding a sense of failure to already soul-crushing pain seemed about as far from a "healing process" model as I could imagine.

As I talked with people about their healing journeys, a new model began to emerge. I asked pointed questions to get at the heart of their circumstances *and* their unique responses. What happened to them? How did they respond? Was their journey progressive in nature? Were there clear steps or stages, or was it more fluid? Did their perspective change over time and, if so, what about it changed? How did they describe the experience at the moment their world changed, a week later, a month later, a year later, or five years later? What steps did they take that were most effective and at what point in their healing journey? At what point did they feel hope that they would one day be happy again? On the way, I became committed to developing a different framework to imagine, model, and understand the grief-progression experience.

Where You Are and Where You're Going

I believe the importance of reframing and understanding our grief-to-happiness journey is analogous to the experience shared in the thrilling book *Nerves of Steel* by former Navy and then commercial airplane pilot Captain Tammie Jo Shults as she recounts her 2018 experience landing a crippled Southwest Airlines Boeing 737. Part of the engine literally exploded twenty minutes after takeoff, and Captain Shults was responsible for the lives of nearly 150 passengers and crewmembers. As the passengers were obviously and understandably terrified, the captain bravely battled through the chaos of the moment, gained control of the plane, and was able to get approval from Philadelphia's air traffic control for an emergency landing. Attempting to reassure her anxious copilot in a moment of great stress, Captain Shults declared, "We're going to Philadelphia."

A flight attendant overheard her statement on the crew's intercom and bravely unbuckled from her crew seat to circulate the assurance among the passengers that they were headed to Philadelphia in hopes of an emergency landing. The book recounts how an almost supernatural calm spread throughout the aircraft as people were exposed to this information. What's interesting is that their circumstances hadn't changed; they were still falling out of the sky, the engine was still in catastrophic failure, and parts of the airplane's exterior and one window were completely missing. The only thing that changed was that they had learned *where they were going* in a time of great fear, uncertainty, and anxiety and that there was *hope* they'd make it after all.

That is precisely the goal of exploring the Survive-Alive-Thrive model together! It is my hope that walking together through this journey will help you better understand where you are and where you're going. Yes, your story is unique, and your circumstances may seem unbearable right now. You might not see any way through the tremendous heartache you're feeling or have experienced in the past. What you're going through is real, and your pain and fears are not only valid but understandable. I know this all too well. But I ask you to take a deep breath and trust in those of us who have gone before you. You are not alone, and through other people's stories and experiences, I hope to encourage you to engage the healing process, discover new coping mechanisms, and again experience happiness and joy.

Survive-Alive-Thrive

So where do you start when putting together a model that allows for and embraces our different faith stories, personalities, temperaments, and backstories? The answer is to set aside the notion of a linear progression of singular emotional responses that are checked off in sequence. In contrast, the Survive-Alive-Thrive model is designed to reimagine our loss-to-hope-to-happiness journey as a series of interconnected circles emanating from a center point of impact. Within each stage are *multiple* emotional responses that can persist, vary, and evolve as we

progress from one stage to the next. The model is intended to help us identify where we are on our journey, show us where we are heading, and connect with others who are having (or have had) similar experiences and responses.

Point of Impact

Imagine dropping a smooth stone onto the surface of a calm pond. There's a gentle, almost elegant impact that creates ripples—and over time a series of interconnecting circles—in the water. We've all seen these images, and they can be quite relaxing visually. Those of us who've been through a traumatic experience may have a hard time picturing our grief in such tranquil terms. Instead, it's frequently described as a more violent and disruptive image, like a meteor crashing into the ocean. However you imagine that moment, the point is to picture your loss hitting the water and turning the still, glasslike surface into a series of circles moving outward from the central point of impact. In this image, the surface of the water represents your life journey, the point of impact represents the moment of your loss, and the interconnected circles emanating outward represent the seasons of healing I want to unpack over the next few chapters.

The further out you go from the initial point of impact, with time and distance, the ripples (like your most visceral responses) may grow less intense and more infrequent, but there are still waves of emotion in the water. Like the waves in an ocean observed from a great distance, this can be misleading. It may look relatively flat but your emotional pain can be just as turbulent and heart-wrenching in the outer circles as it is in the center, even though things may *look* relatively peaceful on the surface.

It's important to note that the circles are interconnected in this model, meaning there is not a linear graduation from one stage to the next. In fact, those of us who have experienced loss report that it is a fluid journey that takes us back and forth through a lifelong emotional journey. Our loss experience may be behind us from a chronological perspective, but it is woven into the fabric of our lives and we'll likely revisit it at various times and in various ways for the rest of our lives.

By reflecting on this model and applying it to your experience, my hope is that you will better understand where you are right now, and you can be reassured there will be happier days ahead. The next few chapters will explore the model's three circles in detail, but I'll start here with a macro view of what makes this model different and more effective in navigating loss.

Survive

The most intense and turbulent times following loss are those closest to the point of impact. This is the season when we're operating in survival mode—when our heart, mind, and soul are in triage. As such, the first circle represents the Survive stage. This is the time frame immediately following our loss when we're still shaking from the impact.

Because it is closest to the initial event, this is where you likely feel the most concentrated force of emotions. Psychologists define this stage as experiencing *acute grief,* and many people I have spoken with have referred to it as a *shellshock* period, when they were simply trying to cope with their loss and brokenness one moment to the next, just as I was following Victoria's death. Regardless of how they manifest in your life, we typically feel the most intense emotions at this stage. For now, the important thing to remember is that this is not what your life will look like *forever*; this is just what it looks like *now*.

Alive

The next circle in the model represents the *Alive* stage, in which the heartache and soul pain experienced so intensely in the Survive stage is transitioning to provide you with the emotional elbow room to start processing your loss. Although life oftentimes requires we reengage far before we feel emotionally ready, we are emerging from the survival experience and trying to cope with life's demands. At some point in this stage, you can begin to understand and address your grief while dealing with the responsibilities and obligations of  the outside world. Psychologists refer to this stage as *integrated grief*, and it will likely come slowly and gradually. There is not a fixed time frame for your grief process to evolve from the Survive to Alive stages, and you should not feel pressure to meet an arbitrary deadline. In fact, the integrated circles of the Survive-Alive-Thrive model serve to illustrate that you may coexist in each season for a period of time or have feelings associated with the Survive stage one day and the Alive stage on another, as your grief transitions from one season to the next. The Alive stage doesn't mean your emotional pain is gone or healed; rather, it is a time when you are resuming activities such as returning to work, church, or school and generally getting back into the routines of life while simultaneously working through the emotional challenges you've experienced from loss.

It's important to note that this transition does not mean you are attempting to forget the person you have lost or that you're ignoring whatever traumatic event has happened. Whether you've suffered the death of a loved one or your life has been turned upside down by a financial catastrophe, medical setback, or the end of a relationship, balancing and reintegrating life responsibilities is emotionally exhausting, stressful, and demanding. Either way, the solution is certainly not putting on a fake happy face and pretending everything's all right. We are acutely aware that everything is *not* the same and that our life has, indeed, changed. Here, then, is the season of our grief process when we are actively caring for and intentionally tending to our emotional, mental, and physical health while also figuring out our place in this strange new world.

Thrive

The outermost circle is the Thrive stage, and this represents the season when our loss—which will always be part of our story—now coexists with a new sense of hope and resolve. This part of the journey is characterized by the realization that you're not just living, but you're actually *enjoying* your life again. You may  have reengaged with close friends or developed new and rich relationships— maybe even a new love interest if you've lost a spouse or been divorced. You have responsibilities and may be enjoying hobbies, commitments, and a new schedule. You can think and talk about the person you lost and smile, remembering the good times without mourning their loss all over again. You're able to transcend the frustrations of caring for a family member and, instead, experience the joy and privilege of serving the needs of someone you love. You can reexperience emotional responses such as sadness in a healthy and appropriate manner when reflecting on your loss or when encountering a poignant reminder such as an anniversary date or holiday memory. And you are able to reflect on the trauma in your past without feeling paralyzing or debilitating stress and anxiety that you may have experienced when much closer to the initial impact. In short, you are living a full and rewarding life.

This may seem a million miles away from where you are right now, but, I promise, you can and will get there. If you need encouragement, please visit www.SurviveAliveThrive.org and review the many real-life stories from people who have started thriving again and wish to share their stories, reach out, give back, and encourage those who are still struggling.

Inclusive and Atomic

Rather than limiting the grief response model to a set of specific and limited emotional responses designed to be checked off in linear fashion, the Survive-Alive-Thrive model is inclusive by design. By *inclusive*, I mean that *multiple and varied* potential emotional responses are included in each stage of the grief journey, many of which can be present in each stage of the healing process. Our emotional responses may lessen in intensity, but they will stay with us throughout our progression, even when achieving emotional happiness in the Thrive stage of your loss journey. This is not a bad thing and is an important concept to visualize in light of the incredibly broad nature of emotional responses that are present and potentially experienced by each of us. While there are debates within the academic and professional psychology communities about the number of emotions a human can experience (for example, a 2017 study at UC Berkeley lists twenty-seven human emotions vs. the traditionally held model of only six[6]), because we are so varied and complex, what makes us truly unique is how these variables coexist and interact in times of loss.

For example, sadness and anxiety are examples of emotional responses we can all experience in times of loss and brokenness. They have the potential to affect each of us. Certain emotional responses are healthy and can lead to happiness and joy, while others can be destructive and have negative consequences. The challenge is to mitigate those that are unhealthy, paralyzing, and destructive and harness the power of those that are positive and healing. For you, one emotion may be more latent or dormant than in a friend or family member going through a similar experience. They may also surface in the same person in one loss situation but not in another. For example, many of the emotional responses I experienced when losing my mother in 2000 were significantly different than when I experienced my wife's death sixteen years later. Those emotional responses, although present during both losses, manifested quite differently and had different levels of intensity and frequency.

6   Katie Avis-Riordan, "There are actually 27 human emotions, new study finds," *Country Living*, September 11, 2017, https://www.countryliving.com/uk/wellbeing/news/a2454/27-human-emotions-new-study/#:~:text=In%20previous%20thought%2C%20it%20was,is%20as%20many%20as%2027.

Atomic in Nature

Have you ever seen a diagram of an atom? There's usually a nucleus made up of tightly packed protons and neutrons at the core, and that nucleus is surrounded by electrons moving in tight oval rotations around the center. There is enormous energy and trapped potential generated when those electrons crash into one another! Now consider what this might look like on our healing journey. In the Atomic Emotional Response Model™ diagram, imagine the varied emotional responses to your loss flying all in, around, and through a self-contained circle just like electrons orbiting a nucleus. Add into the mix the metaphorical "protons" of worldly tasks related to resuming life duties, finances, ongoing relationships, and daily interactions with others. Everything is spinning faster and faster within a finite space. The potential for collisions is clear, and as emotional responses and worldly tasks collide, explosive emotional energy can be released. In the early stages of your grief journey, as your emotions and tasks can feel more compressed and compacted, there is greater potential for even more corresponding impacts and collisions.

Atomic Emotional Response Model™

● = *Emotional Responses*
○ = *Life Tasks and Responsibilities*

The atomic dynamic is not just present in the earliest stage of the grief process but persists throughout each stage of the

Survive-Alive-Thrive model. As you can see in the Atomic Emotional Response by Stage™ diagram, each stage has an atomic nature, but the intensity and frequency of impacting emotional collisions lessen as you progress through the healing journey. A significant contributor to that lessening is the concept of emotional space and time, what I like to call emotional *elbow room*. For example, in the Survive stage, our emotions

Atomic Emotional Response by Stage™

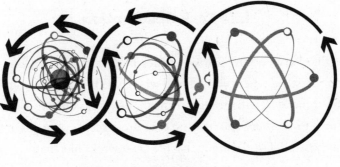

● = Emotional Responses
○ = Life Tasks and Responsibilities

are most intense and packed into a tight timeline filled with daily tasks and responsibilities related to your loss. Think of it as putting ten ping-pong balls in a goldfish bowl and shaking it; there will be a *lot* of collisions in that confined space. As you gain time and distance from your loss event and healing steps are engaged, you have more emotional elbow room to manage life tasks and decisions in less of a pressure-packed timeline. A similar number of emotions and tasks may remain, but now think of those ten ping-pong balls in a larger space such as a storage pod you see outside a home. When shaking the larger container, the emotions are still flying around in an atomic manner, but the space is less confined and the collisions less frequent. In the Thrive stage, your emotional elbow room is even greater, so imagine the contained area is now a hot air balloon! Again, the same number of ping pong balls exists, but they collide much less frequently and with less destructive energy.

In science, we know the potential power of a single atom is mind-blowing. On the grief recovery journey, the potential power of this Atomic Emotional Response "atom" is powerful. The collisions are metaphors for the emotional swings we often experience when processing our loss. They have the power to impact your path to happiness and joy, but you can lessen their impact with the knowledge that they are also a normal and typical part of the grief process.

Life Task Resumption

While the Survive-Alive-Thrive model is designed to enable you to better understand where you are and where you're going on your healing journey, some of us will progress through the circles quickly, while others need more time. There's no rush, no pressure. Except...life doesn't always work like that. In fact, I'd argue that life *never* works like that.

In direct contrast to the healing process, worldly tasks tend to progress in a linear manner, which means the challenges of balancing our daily responsibilities with the healing process are immediately put on the clock. Various life duties require our attention regardless of your loss, some of them requiring immediate attention. Children need their parents—even more so if they're surviving the loss of a mom or dad. Family members in need may continue to require your support. Bereavement leave ends if you're working for an employer. Your home may now be too big or too expensive. There are still bills to pay. You have to go shopping. The meal trains will stop (goodbye, lasagna!). Your son has to go to football practice. Your daughter has soccer practice. Your car needs an oil change. On and on the list goes. You realize quickly that life tasks don't care about your loss or your pain.

To make it more challenging, while in the Survive stage of loss, our capacity for handling and managing even mundane tasks of daily life is at its lowest point on the loss journey. Simply coping with the death of someone you love and planning critical tasks related to their loss is a daunting challenge. In fact, just getting through the next day is sometimes overwhelming. Tragically, this can be the very time we are confronted with the heaviest emotional demands ... and they frequently occur in a condensed time frame.

For example, you could still be in the throes of the Survive stage, just barely hanging on, when your bereavement leave ends (if you have it) and you're expected to return to work. Your boss and colleagues will, no doubt, encourage you to take things slowly the first week, but within a few weeks, it can feel as though they all expect you to perform at the same high level you did before. But you can't; you're still emotionally surviving. How can you be who colleagues expect you to be professionally in the context of where you are in your personal healing journey? These types of life demands add an entirely new and often painful dimension to our recovery process. Even worse, they can lead us to think we should be further along in our healing than we are, causing even more emotional pain. We may think, *It has been six weeks. My life is supposed to be back to normal. Why am I still crying in my pillow at night? What's wrong with me?*

Nothing. Nothing at all.

The problem isn't you. The problem is that your real-world responsibilities have intersected with your emotional healing journey in unrelenting fashion.

Aligning the demands of life with your heart-and-soul healing can often feel like an impossible balancing act—but it *is* possible. And it's not just possible for *other people*; it's possible for *you*. Throughout the rest of this book I'll share strategies from men and women just like you who have met this challenge. I know you can get there too.

Progressive and Persistent

While the Survive-Alive-Thrive model illustrates the inclusive and atomic nature of the emotions we experience in these difficult times of our lives, at the same time it's important to recognize that the nature of the healing journey is also persistent and progressive. As the saying goes, "time and tide wait for no man (or woman)," as life moves along, taking us further and further from the initial point of impact that started our journey. As a matter of fact, the passage of time typically leads to a lessening in both the intensity and frequency of the emotional responses associated with loss. If your loss experience is associated with dealing with a special circumstance (such as divorce or having a sick and/or challenged loved one to care for and manage), you'll likely grow more accustomed to the related obstacles and emotional heartache associated with those responsibilities over time.

That said, the lessening of emotional intensity over time is *not* the same thing as experiencing healing on the journey to achieving long-term happiness and joy. The critical issue is to not confuse the experience of growing accustomed, numbed, or tuned out to those emotions with actually *addressing* those emotions. I have found that the adage "time heals all wounds" is not true when it comes to addressing the heartache associated with loss and can lead to deeper and long-term despair if not addressed in a timely and healthy manner.

In fact, a great majority of the people I've spoken to and interviewed report that, while their emotional responses to loss have persisted over time, their perspective and understanding of those emotions have changed through participating in an intentional healing process. The key here is to understand and embrace the fact that many of the emotions associated with your loss will always be with you and will not magically go away. For example, saying to someone who has lost a child that someday they will no longer feel sadness when remembering them is neither realistic nor healthy. The reality is that there are benchmark birthdates, anniversaries, various activities, certain places, and holidays that connect us to our loved ones. The good news is that you can mitigate the potentially overwhelming and paralyzing emotions and responses by taking positive steps to process your loss. You can nurture those memories and emotions that bring you joy to help you stay in a healthy emotional balance—even while reflecting on and engaging memories of loss.

I can speak from experience here. I've always been an emotional person; it's part of my personality and temperament. Even though I have been blessed to enter a rich new phase of life, having married an incredible and supportive woman, I can still feel sadness over Victoria's death. Why? Because her loss is part of my story and woven into the fabric of my life journey. The fact is that occasional tears or sadness is a perfectly legitimate emotional response to memories related to the death of a loved one, no matter how far removed you are from the initial point of impact. What *would* be cause for alarm, though, is if that sadness still regularly manifested in unhealthy symptoms that made it difficult or impossible to function in my daily life. If you or someone you love is caught or stuck in this situation, I strongly encourage you to connect with a pastor or mental health professional (or both) and attempt to work through the sitation. There is hope. As hard as it may seem right now, don't give up. God loves you and wants to walk with you on the journey to happiness and joy.

Digging Deeper into Survive-Alive-Thrive

In the chapters that follow, my goal is to provide you with some context and understanding of the tools and strategies I and others have used, or are currently using, to process our feelings of grief and brokenness. It is my hope that sharing insights from these stories and personal experiences will help you identify with others and track your journey, while providing steps and resources that can help you work through your loss to find hope and happiness along the way.

At the same time, I want to be clear that there is not a single, magic formula or established timeline for this process. The atomic nature of your loss and the emotions you have experienced are unique to you and your loss, and they are forever woven into the fabric of your life story. I simply hope the Survive-Alive-Thrive model will, first, help you realize that you are not alone and, second, better understand your personal healing journey—whether you are still struggling in the Survive stage or finding joy in the Thrive stage of your life.

Importantly, we will also explore strategies and steps to mitigate the power of *negative* emotional responses while we embrace and nurture the power of *positive* emotional responses. A wide variety of emotions are inherent to our human nature, whether they are presently engaged or dormant. Of course, we want to honestly assess what we're struggling with while building up and focusing on the positive.

Finally, I'll dig deeper into the critical nature of God's role in heart and soul healing and why a relationship with Him as a companion and friend is so important on the path to a joy-filled life.

Now that you know where we're going, let's dig deeper into the seasons of Survive-Alive-Thrive in more detail, drawing on what I've learned from conversations with mental health and counseling professionals, pastors, and, most importantly, real-world survivors across a broad spectrum of loss experiences. First, we'll take a good, hard look at the first stage of loss, when all you can do is hold on tight and do your best to survive.

Questions for Discussion

1. How would you describe your personality? If you've taken a personality inventory, explain the results and discuss how well it describes you.
2. How has your unique personality shaped the way you've experienced loss?
3. How has your backstory shaped the way you've experienced loss?
4. In what ways have you been drawn to others who have experienced loss? Have you been surprised by the types of people with whom you've been most comfortable sharing? Have these people had the same type of loss as you, or have they experienced something very different?
5. What are some of the most intense emotional responses that you've experienced throughout your journey?
6. In what ways have your emotional responses manifested themselves as outward reactions? Consider healthy *and* unhealthy reactions.
7. As we begin to unpack the three stages of the Survive-Alive-Thrive model, what do you expect to discover about yourself and what are your hopeful expectations for each of the three stages?
8. Can you relate to the flood of practical and tactical demands on your time and attention in the aftermath of your loss? What demands have come up throughout your healing journey? How has that affected your ability to fully engage the healing process?
9. How well does the Atomic Emotional Response Model™ describe your healing journey? What collisions have you experienced?

Chapter 6

THE SURVIVE STAGE

PART 1: THE POINT OF IMPACT

AT THE HEART OF THE SURVIVE-ALIVE-THRIVE MODEL IS THE POINT of impact—the moment your world changes—and what I sometimes call "ground zero." This is usually where I begin interviews with people, by asking them to describe their "ground-zero moment." It is often glaringly obvious: It's the phone call from a paramedic, calmly but firmly informing you that your spouse has been in a serious car accident. It's the midnight knock on your door by two police officers who break the news that someone you love is never coming home again. It's the terrifying medical diagnosis in the doctor's office. It's the night your spouse walks out after twenty-five years of marriage. It's the day your loved one moves out of the hospital and into hospice. It's the moment that becomes a dividing line in your life. From now on, you'll think back on your journey through the filter of what happened before this event and what happened after. Whatever loss you've faced, one thing is for certain: your immediate goal is to simply survive.

Where You Are and What You're Facing

In this chapter, we're going to explore three areas related to the Survive stage of the grief process. First, we'll explore three general categories of loss and how they relate and differ from one another. Second, we'll look at two different categories of *circumstances* leading to the death of someone we love that can significantly impact our emotional response. And finally, we'll look at loss in non-death situations that leaves us broken and struggling—things such as being fired, losing a business, experiencing a divorce or broken family relationship, or living in an ongoing situation that is emotionally taxing, such as caring for someone with mental illness or a parent with dementia.

Regardless of the category or root cause of your loss, this chapter will also serve to help identify the unique earmarks of the Survive stage. It's my hope that through this process, you will be able to place yourself in one of the three Survive, Alive, or Thrive stages. This is a good start to connecting with others who see themselves in a similar situation and to taking the actions steps that are proposed in the next chapter.

Finally, I'll review several of the most common challenges associated with this stage of grief and what to expect after the initial moment of impact. The goal is to prepare you for what's ahead on your journey while also helping others in support roles effectively comfort and aid loved ones who are experiencing loss.

Three Categories of Loss

We know from experience that loss comes in a million different shapes and sizes, and it hits from all directions with or without warning. There's no way to list every specific type of loss, but I have organized these experiences into three categories of loss that will sound familiar:

1. **The Midnight Call:** This refers to the sudden, unexpected death of a loved one or any other life-changing tragedy that strikes without warning.
2. **The Long, Hard Road:** This is a loss that occurs slowly over time, most often represented by a loved one's gradual decline and ultimate death by a terminal illness.
3. **Special Circumstances:** This is a day-to-day sense of loss associated not with someone's death but with an ongoing challenge that directly affects your life.

One or more of these types of loss may jump out at you, but let's take a moment to be clear on exactly what we're talking about.

The Midnight Call

Losing someone unexpectedly—literally having them with you one day and gone the next—is an indescribable shock. It is hard to wrap your mind around your entire life changing so much, so fast. That's why I encourage people to make sure they let their loved ones know how much they love them every day. Do not hide your feelings or withhold your love and don't wait for some future day when the stars align to share your heart. I've known too many people who never got the chance they always assumed they'd have.

I've been through it myself and have talked with many people who were happily married at breakfast and grief-stricken widows or widowers by dinner, or they were casually talking with their child in the morning and unable to tuck them into bed that night or any night after. While my wife's death was unexpected and terribly shocking, there are many others I've talked with and interviewed who have shared different versions of this same type of loss. People who have lost spouses to heart attacks, car accidents, or other tragedies. Grieving parents who have lost infants or survived their children's death at the hands of illness, drug overdose, suicide, and accidents. And others who have lost parents, siblings, family members, or good friends to a variety of end-of-life experiences that were heartbreaking and painful to endure. I'll refer to some of these stories in the following chapters, but you can read or listen to these men and women tell their own full stories of loss and healing on our website. Each paints a picture of a loved one's sudden death, and each share how they, family, and friends are coping with unexpected loss. The point of sharing these stories is to connect with the experiences of others and to know you are not alone in your journey.

The Long, Hard Road

If you've walked with a loved one through the long, difficult process of a terminal illness, you know how hard it is to maintain any sense of hope and joy during the battle. It is devastating to watch someone you care about literally wither away before your eyes. Diseases such as cancer, renal failure, amyotrophic lateral sclerosis, (or ALS, commonly known as Lou Gehrig's disease), cystic fibrosis, dementia, and multiple sclerosis all seem so cruel. It can feel impossible to find anything to celebrate as you and your loved ones walk this difficult road. Because this journey usually takes place over months or years, we often think we'll be "ready" when our loved one finally passes from this life into the next. However, we're often still surprised by how hard their death hits us when the time comes and we experience their passing..

Even in such difficult times, there is joy to be found. The thing I've heard most often from people who've walked the long, hard road with a loved one is how glad they were to have had the time to say goodbye. Even though the patient's time is limited, there is at least *some* time for them to put their affairs in order and make sure their families will be taken care of. For their loved ones, there may be time to create new memories, show their love and support, and prepare themselves for life without their spouse, parent, child, family member, or friend. Most importantly, everyone involved may even have the chance to heal broken relationships before it's too late. A terminal diagnosis can put all these things in perspective and remind us of what we too often forget: our time on this earth is limited, and we will have to live the rest of our lives with the decisions we make today.

Interestingly, in talking with people who have lost someone slowly—sometimes agonizingly so—some have wished for a faster outcome to spare all involved from a painful and inevitable death. On the other hand, those who have lost someone suddenly frequently wish they had been granted more time to spend with their loved one before his or her death. They're willing to trade the heartache of watching a slow death for the gift of having just one more day together. I can't tell you how many times I've talked to a survivor of one type of loss who wished or wondered what it would have been like had they experienced the other. The goal is that, over time, we are able to count our blessings, accept the journey as one that cannot be changed, and embrace the positives in our personal experience. I will suggest steps to help achieve that goal in the next chapter.

Special Circumstances

When we speak of loss, we most often think of the grieving process following the *death* of a loved one. However, I know from experience that loss runs far deeper and wider than that. It may seem easy for us to characterize things like a child's physical disability, a spouse's ongoing manic or depressed behavior, a parent's increasing dementia, or a painful divorce as simply "just how life is sometimes." That's true, but it isn't the whole story. The *full* truth is that these things are examples of devastating losses that we feel deeply in our hearts, minds, and spirits. Just like when news of the death of a loved one is received, there is a moment—a point of impact—when we receive news that changes our lives forever. We shouldn't minimize these situations. They can bring about grief and mourning just as strongly as a loved one's death, and, in these cases, we're often doubly burdened by the ongoing care and attention we're required to provide. Without careful management and proper respect, these special circumstances can lead us down a dark road of daily mourning from which we feel there's no escape.

Identifying Ourselves In the Survive Stage

If you've ever been lost inside a shopping mall, you know how helpful the giant map is with the big red star and an arrow that reads, "YOU ARE HERE." There are many, many times in life when we need that kind of clarification, when we have no idea where we are on life's journey. Well . . . the Survive stage is *not* one of those times.

If you're entering the Survive stage, you'll know it. Your entire world has been turned upside down and inside out. Your heart is broken, your mind is splintered, and your body is in shock. Every part of you is struggling to process the loss you've just experienced, and you feel an overwhelming need to keep your head above water. In the very short term, survival is your one and only goal.

While you don't need me to tell you when you're entering the Survive stage, it will still be helpful to identify some of the earmarks of this season. Many of you may be able to consider these experiences in retrospect, having already been through them in your loss process. If you're just now entering this stage, this may help you find your footing and connect with the challenges listed as you begin your healing journey.

SURVIVE STAGE OVERVIEW

HALLMARKS OF THE STAGE	WHAT THAT CAN MEAN/LOOK LIKE
1 ATOMIC CHAOS	Close proximity to loss event
	Struggling with emotions
	Vulnerability
2 EMOTIONALLY OVERWHELMING	Numbness, sense of shock or disbelief
	Desire to help others while you're struggling
	Juggling emotions with practical responsibilities
	Besieged with major decisions while mourning
3 FORGETFULNESS / BEWILDERMENT	Feeling like you're in a fog
	Challenging to focus on basic tasks
	Struggling to stay on topic in conversations

Hallmark 1: Atomic Chaos

The Survive stage is, without a doubt, the most emotionally charged part of your journey. In the previous chapter, we saw how the Atomic Emotional Response Model™ represents the densely packed nature of the numerous emotions and daily tasks we are confronted with at the time of our most intense grief. In light of the compressed timeline of

● = *Emotional Responses*
○ = *Life Tasks and Responsibilities*

this stage and the numerous responsibilities that demand our attention at this point in our journey, the Survive stage is the most emotionally dynamic season by far.

During this period, the emotional struggle you're dealing with is overlaid with urgent, practical tasks and decisions that must be taken care of immediately. You have more things going on in your life, more decisions to make, more significant and weighty life-altering issues to address than any other time. Additionally, all these things are crashing down on you during the time when you are most broken and vulnerable. Even worse, you will live with these decisions for the rest of your life, and you are definitely feeling the pressure to do everything the *right* way—even though you don't have the time to give these decisions the deep consideration you normally would.

When you add in your unique personality's response to stress, the potential for this new loss to reignite old pain, and how this loss fits within your faith framework and worldview, let's just say there are going to be some atomic collisions. Don't be surprised when, just as you exclaim, "I can't take one more surprise or demand!" you get hit with ten new surprises and demands. I'm afraid that's just how this season works. This is one reason why it is so important to identify your community of friends and family members who are ready, willing, and able to jump in and help. I know I would not have made it through the Survive stage without them.

It's important to note that after spending time with those who have lost a loved one and do not have a close circle of friends or family to lean on for support, I know it can be devastating to try and walk the journey on your own. If you are struggling and without a support network, please visit our website www.Survive-Alive-Thrive.org and join a virtual grief group. We offer support and resources to help you on your journey. Please know that you are not alone!

Hallmark **2**: Emotionally Overwhelming

In the midst of taking care of myriad practical matters, you're also dealing with the fact that your emotions are completely overloaded. And, as you no doubt discover, so are everyone else's. This is an emotionally volatile time, and arguments are common among the grieving people left behind in the wake of a shared loss. If you are the one most impacted and most responsible for the planning in the immediate aftermath, you can expect the added burden of becoming a caregiver to others who have been impacted by this loss. For example, when my wife died, I was struggling to stay sane and keep my emotions in check. However, I still found myself having to comfort others who were mourning Victoria's death. My entire world had fallen apart, and yet I found myself consoling others.

This is another area where varying personalities make a big difference in how we experience loss. It is hard to understand why someone is reacting the way they are if you're coming at it from a completely different perspective. If you're a more introverted and reserved person, you'll likely keep your emotions in check when you're around others. However, if your best friend is more extroverted and open with her feelings, you could easily be troubled by a reaction that seems downright hysterical to you. Or if you're the one who is freer with your emotions and your friend is stoic, you might be hurt by her apparent indifference to your loss.

We'll discuss some strategies for working through this emotional web in the following chapter. For now, it's enough to caution you against judging another's emotional reactions to loss. We all go through the Survive stage a little differently because we're all wired differently.

Hallmark ❸: Forgetfulness and Bewilderment

Survive is generally marked by a sense of bewilderment. This is different from absentmindedness, which we'll discuss in a different stage. As you progress through the healing journey, you may also experience periods of forgetfulness. Many people describe the feeling as though they are working through a deep fog. Even when you *think* you can think and see things clearly, you're really just squinting to make out shapes in the darkness. You may forget things—from funeral details to where you parked your car to your best friend's name. This is not the time to be making life-altering decisions, and yet it is precisely when we're called on to do just that. I strongly encourage you to delay any significant decision that isn't urgent at this point, and I further recommend running necessary decisions past a trusted friend or mentor during this season. No, you aren't seeking someone's *permission*; you're just providing yourself a trusted second opinion to catch yourself from making a big mistake during a time when you need a little mental backup.

Specific Challenges of the Survive Stage

While every stage of the Survive-Alive-Thrive model is filled with challenges, the Survive stage feels more intense due to the short time frame associated with many of the decisions required. There's no way I can list *every* challenge you'll face during this stage, but I do want to highlight several that you should expect. In doing so, hopefully this can either give you a heads-up on some things you'll likely face or at least give you the comfort of knowing you're not alone in what you're dealing with right now.

NOTABLE CHALLENGES OF THE SURVIVE STAGE	
NOTABLE CHALLENGES	WHAT THAT CAN MEAN/LOOK LIKE
1 COMPACT NATURE OF DECISIONS	Decisions coming hard and fast
	Incredible sense of responsibility
	Have to live with the decisions for the rest of your life
	Emotional pushback from others
2 URGENT MEDICAL DECISIONS	Managing organ donation
	Potential for an autopsy
	How to handle the remains
3 HOSPITAL AND POLICE REQUIREMENTS	Identifying the body
	Endless paperwork
	Police investigation and reports

NOTABLE CHALLENGES	WHAT THAT CAN MEAN/LOOK LIKE
4 ESTATE AND LEGAL ISSUES	Did the person have a living will?
	Finding the will or estate plan
	Procuring death certificates
	Closing financial accounts
5 PLANNING THE MEMORIAL SERVICE	Deciding on burial vs. cremation
	Choosing a casket or urn
	Finding the best time that accommodates people's schedules
6 MANAGING FRIENDS, FAMILY, AND OFFERS OF HELP	Selecting a "gatekeeper"
	Showing gratitude during grief
	Accepting help from others
7 HANDLING HURTFUL COMMENTS	People *will* say some insensitive things to you
	Showing grace when people don't know what to say

Challenge **1**: Compact Nature of Decisions

Whenever someone you love and are responsible for dies, decisions will come flying at you hard and fast. You may get a dozen or more phone calls in the first twenty-four hours from different offices and agencies needing exhaustive information from you. You'll be making decisions on the fly that you may have to live with for the rest of your life, and this can cause many people to completely shut down. Plus, if others in your family disagree with your decision, you'll also have to deal with their emotional pushback (and possibly blame) as well.

Challenge ❷: Urgent Medical Decisions

You may have been shocked by how many medical decisions you had to make immediately following a loved one's death. Here are just a few of the medical issues that I and others have experienced during this heart-wrenching time:

- **Organ Donation:** I'll never forget the thirty-minute phone call I had with the organ donation service mere hours after my wife took her life. In the midst of my shock and grief, I was forced to spend a half hour on the phone talking to a stranger about my wife's complete medical history. There were questions I wouldn't have been able to answer on my *best* day, let alone hours after losing my wife of over twenty years. And then, after an endless list of questions, I was told that Victoria wasn't a candidate for organ donation due to a health issue in her history. It was excruciating. Of course, I fully support organ donation and I think it is a wonderful way to bless another person with the gift of life. My own mother was granted a sixteen-year new lease on life because of the generous donation of another person's kidney, so I've seen the blessings firsthand. However, the actual phone call and questionnaire in my darkest moment was a hardship I never saw coming and wouldn't wish on anyone. For that reason, I recommend that families have serious conversations about their decision to become an organ donor rather than simply clicking a box at the DMV when getting your license. It is a beautiful gift, but it is a gift that comes at a cost to those grieving your loss. Go into this with your eyes open. And be sure to research the requirements for a donor. If you have an ongoing health issue such as diabetes, they can't accept or take your organs, so you can spare your loved ones the heartache of having to go through a post-death phone call like I had. If you are healthy enough to qualify as a donor, have that discussion with the loved one most likely to be the decision-maker at your time of death so they will know your wishes and intent.

- **Autopsy:** Another challenge you may face is the question of an autopsy. We often think of this only in cases of foul play, but there are other reasons you may choose to have an autopsy performed. If there are any questions about why the person died, an autopsy may give you the answers you need to close that chapter of your experience. It could also be a way to contribute to scientific research and thereby help others. This is actually a decision I had to make when Victoria died. Because her mental health issues arose following multiple car accidents, I was interested to know if CTE—chronic traumatic encephalopathy—played a role. This is a relatively new field of research primarily centered around athletes who are at risk for repeated brain injuries and victims of car accidents who subsequently experience mental or emotional health disorders. I was fortunate to have my sister, a physician, help me quickly identify resources for this procedure, but most people are left to explore the options on their own.

- **Handling the Remains:** Of course, there is also the issue of how to handle the body post-mortem. You're forced to answer questions about burial, where to have the body sent, and what your expectations are for its preparation. Or you may choose cremation and face a whole different set of questions, especially if your faith frowns on this. Again, this is something you want to be as clear as possible with *before* your death, so your survivors know exactly what your wishes are *after* your death.

If you think your medical decisions will end with your loved one's death, you need to reset your expectations. The questions you'll get after their passing will be just as difficult as the ones before.

Challenge ❸: Hospital and Police Requirements

Depending on how your loved one died, you will likely have to work with the hospital and police to varying degrees on:

- **Identifying the Body:** You may be required to identify your loved one's body, which can be a terrible burden. Some people appreciate this last opportunity to see the person, while others only want to remember them alive. The image of a loved one's lifeless body is something you will never forget, so go into these situations mindfully. The decision will literally be with you for the rest of your life.

- **Endless Paperwork:** There is quite a bit of paperwork involved with a loved one's passing, so you can expect to sign many, many forms at the hospital. You might also be called upon to collect the person's belongings, especially if they died suddenly.

- **Police Investigation and Reports:** The police will often be involved in a death. Of course, they are on the scene of a car accident or other public incident to manage traffic and perform an accident investigation. They will also be quite active in cases of suicide or any death that occurs under mysterious or criminal circumstances. It is a natural reaction to recoil from the types of questions these officers are required to ask, but we must remember these men and women are doing a very important job. It's their duty to ensure our loved one's death is properly investigated and documented, and, when necessary, to make sure justice is done in the event of a wrongful death. I know this firsthand, as I had to watch several officers search my own house for a suicide note and, I'm certain, signs of foul play the night Victoria died.

In my experience, the hospital staff and police officers were patient, kind, and respectful, but they had a job to do and I had to give them the space and cooperation to do it. They will expect the same of you.

Challenge ④: Estate and Legal Issues

I don't want to sound insensitive, but the truth is that every death comes with a mountain of legal paperwork, forms, and red tape. Those include:

- **Living Will:** In the best cases, the legal process starts with the deceased's living will. This is a legal document that outlines exactly what lifesaving measures the person wants for him-/ herself in the event of a life-threatening accident or medical situation. I cannot stress enough how important this is for every adult reading this. A living will is a gift of love you give your family when they need it the most. It saves them from having to take responsibility for your life-support decisions. When the individual's wishes are clearly stated beforehand and documented in a living will, the remaining family members are spared the burden of those life-and-death decisions and the familial infighting that goes along with them.

  This is especially relevant to my family. Sadly, just five weeks following my remarriage, my new mother-in-law suffered a terrible accident that resulted in critical brain injuries. With her mentally incapacitated, we relied on her clear living will, which she drafted ten years previously, to make sure we followed her wishes for her own health. Because her living will stated she did not want to be kept alive through artificial means, we were spared the burden of deciding whether to keep her on life support in the hospital or move her into hospice to let nature take its course. We moved her into our home for her final days of hospice, and she died peacefully surrounded by family. Despite our sense of loss, we are at peace knowing we did exactly what she wanted, and we were able to give her comfort for her last days rather than spend them fighting amongst ourselves about how long to try to keep her alive.

- **Will or Estate Plan:** Hopefully, the loved one who has passed had a will outlining their wishes for their estate and belongings. If not, you'll likely face a tough road trying to close out their estate. Regardless, it can be an emotionally charged process to sort through and separate the business and financial side of the obligations from the heartache and pain you are experiencing at this stage in your loss journey.

- **Death Certificates and Closing Accounts:** You'll also need to deal with death certificates and power of attorney documents, and you'll probably have to make sure their banks and creditors have the information and documentation they need to settle their accounts properly. Much of this may be more difficult if you don't know the person's financial institutions, account numbers, passwords, and so on.

Take this as an urgent suggestion to get your estate and related paperwork together as soon as possible; you are blessing your loved ones if you've taken steps to ensure your executor knows everything they need to know about your estate in the event of your death.

Challenge ⑤: Planning the Memorial Service

The memorial service for Victoria was held ten days following her death. That period was chaotic and painful. It was full of challenges associated with her suicide, the planning of the service, dealing with family, handling medical decisions, and much more. I was holding onto the raft as it cascaded down the rapids, trying not to be thrown emotionally overboard. And yet, at the same time, I had to decide how I and everyone we knew would pay our final respects to my wife.

Things you'll need to decide at this point include:

- Burial or cremation?
- Open or closed casket?

- Which casket or urn?
- Which photos best capture your loved one's life and should be present at the service?
- Where should the service be held?
- Will there be a separate memorial service and graveside service?
- Will you have a time of visitation before the memorial service?
- Who should officiate? Who else should speak?
- What music should you play?
- When can/should/will the service be held, and who will/won't be able to make it on that day?

Of all the questions you're likely to face, that last one—*when*—may be the most problematic. It's impossible trying to time these events around everyone's schedules, and there will certainly be people who can't make it on the day you choose. This can cause bitterness and resentment among family members, but you cannot accommodate everyone. Plus, there may be circumstances beyond your control that dictate how, when, and where you can hold memorial services. For example, as this book was written, the country was still reeling from the COVID-19 pandemic. In some cases, people who lost family members were not able to hold memorial services for their loved ones for several months. This inability to attain closure by celebrating a lost loved one's life was significantly painful for many, many people.

Challenge **6**: Managing Friends, Family, and Offers of Help

In previous chapters, I discussed my struggles dealing with all the well-meaning friends and family members who reached out to me after my wife's death. Everyone wanted to talk, but I wasn't mentally or emotionally able to talk to many people for several days. That's when I relied on my sister as my gatekeeper—and why I recommend every person going through the Survive stage ask someone to be their own gatekeeper. I also mentioned my hesitancy to accept the many offers of help that people gave, including my church's offer to provide meals for me and my son. Again, my sister stepped in and saved the day on that issue, convincing me that I did indeed need the help.

I won't restate all the challenges involved with navigating the vast sea of friends and family during this difficult time, but I will encourage you to revisit my story—particularly the "Dealing with Friends and Family" section of chapter 3—to better understand many of the difficulties you're likely to face in this area.

Challenge ⑦: Handling Hurtful Comments

As I've said before, even the most well-meaning people are going to say some shockingly insensitive things to you as you wade through the Survive waters. I've heard more than my share of well-intentioned but hurtful things and have focused on this topic in grief groups I've facilitated. In one group session, I shared a particularly thoughtless question from a neighbor weeks after Victoria's memorial service. While bumping into my son and I as we were shopping for produce in the supermarket, his question about her death was inappropriate and shocking. Once the group had progressed past the initial shock of the question he'd posed, many others shared similar anecdotes. In that setting, the more stories shared, the more we had to laugh at the nature of the experiences. Turns out that it was therapeutic to listen to others and realize we were not alone in this regard. *Almost.* It's my belief that in most instances, people simply don't know what to say, and what eventually falls out of their mouths is said with the best intention and, regrettably, with the least thought. Pair that with the fact that many people are uncomfortable sitting in silence, and you're sure to hear some painful, stupid things from the people you love and trust the most. Prepare for it. It's *going* to happen. However, I have some suggestions for how to deal with this and how to avoid being the one saying dumb things. You'll see those in the following chapter in the "Dos and Don'ts" recommendations section.

The Weight of the World

As you have read, there is a daunting list of challenges and tasks you can be confronted with while struggling in the immediate aftermath of losing a loved one. The start of our healing journey is covered in pain, anguish, and a terrifying sense of helplessness. Surviving is not easy when your heart is broken and the weight of the world is pressing down on you. This is a particularly challenging time of life, when we're trying to cope with our loss, identify what needs to be done quickly, and understand what exactly we're feeling and experiencing.

I cannot overstate how important it is to take this season seriously, giving yourself time and freedom to process your loss and manage the tasks that have been thrust upon you. In the following chapter, we will continue our discussion of the Survive stage by examining emotional responses and outward reactions that occur during this stage and review some practical steps for getting through this stage in a healthy way. Plus, I'll give you some suggestions for how you can care for others going through this difficult time with grace and wisdom.

Questions for Discussion

1. "Ground zero" is described as the initial point of impact, the moment your world changes forever. Describe your "ground-zero moment."

2. Which type of loss—the midnight call, the long, hard road, or special circumstances—best describes your experience? Have you ever wished you had a different type of loss experience (i.e., having more time to say goodbye if you lost someone suddenly, wishing your loved one had died quickly rather than suffering for a long time, and so on)?

3. If your loss was from special circumstances, was it medical, mental health, emotional health, or something else entirely? Have you faced any stigmas surrounding your circumstances?

4. If your loss has left you in the role of caregiver for a loved one, describe your new responsibilities. How has this new role changed your life? What is your expectation for the future?

5. Describe the pressure you felt in the immediate aftermath of your loss, as you had to face the mounting demands of life. What were some of your biggest challenges and failures as you attempted to manage all these things at the most pressure-filled time of your life?

6. This chapter listed a few earmarks of the Survive stage. Which of these most resonated with you? Why? What other earmarks would describe your Survive experience?

7. What is the biggest challenge you are facing or have faced during Survive?

8. If your loss involved a loved one's death, describe your mindset going into the memorial service. What decisions did you have to make? What would you have done differently?

9. What legal issues surprised you as you entered this stage? How have you overcome them?

10. What are some of the insensitive things well-meaning people have said to you during this time? How did you react? (Hint: it's okay to laugh at them!)

Chapter 7

THE SURVIVE STAGE

Part 2: First Steps on the Healing Journey

YOUR WORLD IS DIFFERENT. THE LOSS YOU HAVE BEEN THROUGH IS still close at hand and sometimes you find yourself struggling even to form a coherent thought. You're in shock, and in a matter of weeks, days, or even hours, this shock gives way to a wide range of coping mechanisms—behaviors, responses, and reactions born out of our trauma. It can be difficult to anticipate exactly how we'll respond in our time of loss because our responses are so deeply personal. We react in ways that are influenced by our unique personalities, backstories, and faith/worldviews. Those factors are the lenses through which we try to understand, experience, and process our loss, and the resulting coping mechanisms that emerge can be surprising—both to ourselves and to the people trying to love us through our pain.

You didn't ask for this change. It was an unwelcome interruption to the life you had before your loss came crashing through the door. But it's here now. It's part of your life, and it isn't going away. Whether you want to or not, you must begin the healing journey. You must gather what little strength of will and spirit you have and face the hard days ahead. On some days, your number one goal each morning will be to simply make it through one more day. If you can just make it one more day, you may tell yourself, you'll be doing great.

The good news is, you are not alone. I'm right here with you, and so is a vast community of men and women who have been right where you are now. I'll discuss how to connect with others through grief groups and online communities later, but, for now, my goal is to help you better understand your experience, mitigate the anxiety and stress you are feeling, and help you better respond and react to the pressure you're now facing.

What to Expect in This Chapter

In this chapter we're going to review various common emotional reactions and how they can manifest in our grieving process. While we all have a set of unique responses and experiences, we'll explore similar responses we can share across age, gender, category, and type of loss. The goal is to identify your own personal experience and to embrace the idea that you are not alone in what you're going through. While we do not necessarily experience all the responses listed, nor do we need to, there are likely some with which you can relate.

I will also recommend strategies and healthy steps to empower you to process and manage your grief on the path to hope and healing. The suggestions provided are aggregated from my own personal experiences—from spending the past several years talking with and interviewing others who have been through loss and brokenness—and from input from pastors and mental health professionals. It's my hope and prayer that you will find ideas that can help you as you progress through your healing journey.

Finally, I will also give suggestions for those who are not going through loss *themselves*, but who are supporting someone they love through it. It has been estimated that 200 million Americans are directly affected by the loss of a friend or family member each year, and this was *before* the COVID-19 pandemic, which has affected us *all*. Of that number, there are many of us who are simply trying to be of service and support. We'll discuss a few dos and don'ts that can help you avoid adding to the grief experience and aid you in providing the comfort that is so deeply needed and appreciated.

Definitions Related to Healing Experience

As we explore various experiential aspects of the healing journey, let's review a couple of key terms we'll use throughout the upcoming chapters. These will make it easier to understand how and why we experience loss and healing in such a personal manner:

- **Faith/Worldview:** This represents your foundational belief system and how you see the world. If you're a Christian or a practicing member of another faith, your worldview is likely centered on or greatly influenced by your relationship with or understanding of God. If not, while the world offers many options to consider, it is my hope this book will encourage you to consider how your loss experience can be impacted through the companionship of a present and loving God.

- **Backstory:** While your faith/worldview is about what you believe and the filter through which you perceive your place in the journey of life, your backstory is about what you have been through. This is your unique, personal history, full of accomplishments, setbacks, tragedies, and joyful experiences. How you were raised, your relationship with your parents and family, and current and previous relationships and past traumas are all represented here. It's the patchwork of experiences that make up your life story.

- **Personal Blueprint:** This refers to your unique blend of variables, including your backstory, faith/worldview, personality, temperament, and genetic predisposition that all work together to influence how you react to and experience loss. It is effectively a "goulash" of your genetic characteristics and your emotional, intellectual, and environmental experiences. Simply put, it's the combination of your *nature* and your *nurture*.

- **Emotional Responses:** This describes how you respond at an emotional level to the challenges and circumstances we are thrust into. For example, in the case of a painful loss, you will likely experience sadness. On the other hand, if you won the lottery, you would likely experience the emotional response of elation. I'll review a wide range of emotional responses in the coming chapters and how they have been experienced by others who have gone through loss.

- **Response Manifestations:** This represents how your emotional responses are outwardly demonstrated in your life. For example, the emotional response of elation after winning the lottery can present itself in several different ways, including laughter or even tears. On the other hand, the emotional response of sorrow following the loss of a loved one could manifest itself as an emotional outburst, such as crying or silence and withdrawal. There is no right or wrong, as the manifestations of our emotional responses are unique to each of us and driven by the variables that make up our Personal Blueprint (as defined above).

So Much, So Fast

Everything in the Survive stage happens way too fast. As we saw in the previous chapter, this is the most tightly packed, unrelenting, demanding, and explosive season of the Survive-Alive-Thrive model. The closer you are to the point of impact, the more overwhelming everything feels and the greater the pressure to make substantial decisions in tight time frames. If someone you love has passed away, you know what those first two weeks look like. Not only are your dealing with the emotional whirlwind of grief and shock, but you're also called on to make incredibly important decisions that you'll live with for the rest of your life. Medical decisions such as organ donations and autopsies require immediate time-sensitive decisions. Police inquiries, hospital paperwork, funeral arrangements, memorial service planning, and more are in need of your direction—and that's in addition to trying to stay on top of all your normal responsibilities such as caring for children, paying bills, shopping, and workplace demands.

Life usually gives us a week or two to grapple with our initial emotional responses and make these life-changing decisions, and that's not nearly enough time. Survive calls us to act decisively, immediately, and boldly at a time when all we want to do is curl up in a ball and hide. I wish I could make that easier for you, but you know I can't. The best I can do is give you space not only to feel what you're feeling, but to understand *why* you're feeling it and what you can *do* with it. And hopefully, I can follow that with some practical steps for getting through this season with your sanity intact.

Survive Emotional Responses to Loss

In my work with different grief groups and through interviews with survivors, I've identified several different emotional responses and outward reactions we might expect during the Survive stage. Keep in mind, however, that these are *possible* responses; I'm not saying you will experience all of these, and I'm not suggesting you'll work through them in any particular order or according to any timetable. That kind of forced and anticipated linear progression doesn't work in real life—at least in my experience (or for any of the people I've worked with).

Instead, you might experience any or all of these responses. And you might find relief from their sting in a matter of weeks. Or it might take months. Or years. Or longer. And the pain from one response—anger at a doctor's initial misdiagnosis, for example—might fade in time only to flare up unexpectedly two, ten, or twenty years later. What you experience on Day 2 may be totally different than what you feel on Day 3, Day 30, or Day 180. The point is that these responses are messy; they don't follow any rules, and our goal isn't to control, master, or "get over" any of them. Rather, our goal here—especially in this Survive stage—is simply to recognize them and give ourselves a safe place to experience our natural responses to a heartbreaking loss. For now, think of it less as a road map and more of a roll call. We're not telling our reactions where to go; at this stage, we're just trying to recognize and better understand what responses we're dealing with.

SURVIVE STAGE: EMOTIONAL RESPONSE SNAPSHOT

EMOTIONAL RESPONSE	WHAT THAT CAN MEAN/LOOK LIKE
1 **Shock, Numbness, and Disbelief**	Your brain seems to shut down
	Unable to process what's happening moment to moment
	Grief ebbs and flows wildly
2 **Emotional Outbursts**	Prone to uncharacteristic emotional outbursts
	Weeping at the drop of a dime
	Don't know why you're crying
	Can't understand why you're so emotional
3 **Powerlessness and Frustration**	Maddening to be unable to stop the loss
	Helplessness when the outcome is clear and unavoidable
	Feel at the mercy of whatever Survive throws at you

EMOTIONAL RESPONSE	WHAT THAT CAN MEAN/LOOK LIKE
4 **Anger and Impatience**	Mood changes hour to hour
	Inability to tolerate other people's quirks
	No patience
	Random flashes of anger

Response **1**: Shock, Numbness, and Disbelief

Nearly every person I've interviewed has used the word *shock* or *stunned* to describe their initial reaction to the loss. They just couldn't believe it. There's a cognitive dissonance wherein our brains simply can't process the conflict between our old and new realities. The night Victoria died, for example, I remember being surrounded by police officers, paramedics, pastors, and friends in my house and saying from time to time, "This can't be happening" or, "How could this happen?" or some variation on that theme. *Shock* doesn't even begin to capture what we feel in these moments, but it's the best word we have to describe it. And yet, at the same time, we're called on to make immediate decisions or answer a long list of questions. Unreal.

Sometimes it's like being trapped underwater and hearing the faint, unintelligible murmur of people talking around you. Then your head occasionally pops to the surface in a moment of lucidity and you zero in on what someone's saying to you. Your mind races to catch up as you say something like, "Huh? I'm sorry, what were you saying? The hospital needs me to do what?" A friend patiently explains (again) what the hospital needs you to do and your head slips back beneath the surface. The darkness and senseless murmuring envelops you once again. It can be all too much.

Throughout Survive—and especially in the immediate aftermath of the loss—your grief will ebb and flow. One moment, you'll feel fine and you'll be able to answer direct questions, make decisions, and focus on what others are thinking and feeling. The next moment, you'll find yourself in a puddle of tears and unable to even speak. You have no control over where these emotional swings will take you or when they will come. As brutal and overwhelming as this experience is, this is a common response at this stage of the journey. Remember that you are not alone; millions of us have been there as you may have been.

Response ②: Emotional Outbursts

During Survive, we are most prone to often-uncharacteristic emotional outbursts, including unexpected bouts of weeping, irritability, or moments of anger. I've talked to many people—especially men—in the first few weeks after a terrible loss who were confused about how they were acting. It's not uncommon for otherwise "big, tough guys" to become so overwhelmed with emotion that they can't stop crying. I can't tell you how many times I've heard people say something such as, "What's wrong with me? Why am I feeling this way? I've never been like this before. Why do I keep crying out of nowhere?"

Well, it's not "out of nowhere." Rather, you're reacting out of your grief. Tremendous loss brings a tremendous emotional response, and that response very often includes unexpected fits of tears—even for tough guys and gals.

A good friend once told me about how he broke down crying in a nursing home because his mother wanted strawberry ice cream instead of the rocky road he'd just brought her. On the surface, that sounds like a massive overreaction. When you know the full story, though, it makes much more sense. You see, his mother had always *loved* rocky road ice cream. It was her favorite by a mile. He'd had a lifetime of memories having wonderful, intimate conversations with his mother over a bowl of rocky road. Later in life, she developed Alzheimer's and had to be put into a long-term care facility. One day, he thought he'd surprise her with a treat, so he picked up some rocky road and went for a visit. He came into her room and proudly said, "Hey, Mom! I brought you some rocky road—your favorite!"

She looked up at him with confusion in her eyes. "Rocky road? Oh, I *hate* rocky road. You know that. I wanted strawberry. That's always been my favorite."

My friend excused himself and stepped out to the hallway, where he burst into tears. For him, this wasn't about ice cream; it was about a moment of great loss, realizing his mother was gone. Her illness had slowly eaten away at her memories, taking much of her personality with it. The woman who was left was a stranger to him, and his heart was broken. So ... he wept.

The Survive stage brings many unexpected emotional triggers, and we can't anticipate how we'll respond to each one. My advice here is simple: be patient with yourself. You may not know *why* you're crying, but you honestly don't *need* to know why. If you're weeping, it's because your heart needs to weep.

Response ❸: Powerlessness and Frustration

Another response that is common for most people, whether they are action-oriented or idea-oriented, is general feelings of powerlessness and frustration. It is incredibly frustrating—if not outright maddening—to watch a loved one go through unimaginable pain and suffering up to and including death, and yet not be able to help them. This is what you feel when the doctor who has looked after your ailing parent finally says, "I'm sorry. There's nothing more we can do." And it's certainly what you feel when you get the midnight call that someone you love has died and you didn't even get a chance to say goodbye. We want so badly to *do something*, to be the hero, to save the day. But most of the time, we simply can't ... and that is a very hard reality to handle.

A woman I interviewed who lost her husband to cancer told me about all the different homeopathic and nutritional things they tried to stave off the cancer, including radical changes in diet, improvements to the house air and water filtration systems, and more. Their aggressive approach worked for a while and the cancer seemed to be regressing, but then one of the tests came back and showed two little nodules of regrowth. It was devastating and frustrating. Moving forward, her husband refused all additional treatments and died soon thereafter.

Talking about her sense of powerlessness at that point, she reflected on accepting her husband's decision to stop treatment, despite all they'd done together, and all the work and research she had done in an attempt to help save his life. He needed to be at peace and she reluctantly accepted his decision, sitting with him and holding him as he took his last breath.

Survive drags us along kicking and screaming. We have more agency, more ability to positively impact our situation in Alive and Thrive, but we can feel totally at the mercy of whatever Survive throws at us. For many of us, that sense of powerlessness is one of the most difficult and frustrating parts of the process.

Response ➍: Anger and Impatience

Because your emotions are always going up and down, and because those emotions are constantly crashing into your old responsibilities and new, urgent demands, you might find your mood changing hour to hour. You may also lose the ability to tolerate other people's personality characteristics, leading you to snap at people you normally get along with. Your patience is at an all-time low here because you are using every ounce of emotional, mental, and physical energy simply to survive the loss you've experienced and because you're most likely not sleeping well. Random flashes of anger, resentment, frustration, irritation, and impatience should be expected.

I spoke to a woman days after the death of her mother. The family had just held the memorial service, and she was surprised at how angry she felt about some family members' attitude and behavior throughout the hospice, death, and funeral experiences. She had moved her mother into her home and cared for her in her final days. Family members had been in and out of the house, but there were some who seemed removed and few seemed as invested in what was happening as she was. It was a struggle to get everyone to pitch in, and her frustration built up over what she perceived as cold indifference by some for what her mother was going through and, honestly, what she was going through herself. When her mother passed, some family members objected to the suggested date for the memorial service due to vacation plans or graduation parties that couldn't move. From her perspective, it seemed everyone had other things they considered to be more important, and she finally snapped.

These types of emotional responses are common due to the atomic nature of the grief process. When we're tired, stressed, anxious, grieving, heartbroken, scared, confused, lonely, and feeling powerless, we're primed to burst in unexpected fits of anger. This, I believe, is why many families can suffer breakdowns after the death of a beloved matriarch or patriarch. The sad reality is that a death can send emotional shockwaves that can devastate families and communities if we aren't careful.

Suggested Steps for Healing Progression

I said in the previous chapter that no one will have to tell you when you're in the Survive stage. Believe me, you'll know. So far, we've examined several earmarks of Survive, as well as a laundry list of challenges and painful emotional responses we can expect. But the big question is, what can we do to actually *survive* Survive? The following list provides some healthy steps for navigating the Survive stage and to get started on your journey to healing.

HEALTHY STEPS: NAVIGATING THE *SURVIVE* STAGE	
HEALTHY STEPS	WHAT THAT CAN MEAN/LOOK LIKE
1 Lean on Your Faith	Believe in miracles again
	Focus on blessings
	Trust God and be grateful for His grace

HEALTHY STEPS	WHAT THAT CAN MEAN/LOOK LIKE
❷ Care for Your Mental Health	Your emotional and mental health are paramount in Survive What you do now may dictate the kind of life you have later
❸ Get Help	Make sure you aren't going through this alone You need people now more than ever Don't be afraid to ask for help
❹ Explore Music as Therapy	Music captures the deep longings of our hearts Play songs that meant something to your loved one
❺ Get Off the Sofa	Engage in physical activity Exercise gives you physical stamina for the trying days ahead Exercise is a natural antidepressant
❻ Be Honest about How You Feel	This is not the time to put on a brave face Burying our feelings never works
❼ Share with Others	Sharing with others helps us be honest with ourselves There is comfort in sharing
❽ Celebrate Happy Memories	Give yourself permission to enjoy memories Sharing stories with others helps everyone celebrate the person you lost

HEALTHY STEPS	WHAT THAT CAN MEAN/LOOK LIKE
9 Show Grace to Others	People around you will make mistakes Be patient with others as they try to serve you
10 Access Online Resources	Join a virtual grief group or discussion Listen to a podcast story related to your loss

Step **1**: Lean on Your Faith

If you're a person of faith, do not let this experience derail your relationship with God. Instead, run to Him for comfort and support. He is still there, and He still does miracles. Especially if your loved one suffered a long, hard road, you can be comforted in the assurance that he or she is safe and healed in the arms of a loving God. There are many more blessings to be found in even these dark times, and we will discuss them at length in section 3 of this book.

Step **2**: Care for Your Mental Health

Protecting your emotional and mental health is paramount while fighting through the first stage of the Survive-Alive-Thrive model. It will seem like everything is working against your emotional health and stability at this point, which makes it more important than ever to stay on top of things and proactively care for yourself. The following steps will certainly help, but right now the most important thing you can do is to constantly remind yourself that the attention you give yourself now, during Survive, will dictate what kind of life you will have moving forward. I know that sounds dramatic, but it's true. You *have* to make your mental and emotional health a priority right now.

Step ❸: Get Help

First and foremost, make sure you are not going through this alone. You need people more at this stage than you have ever needed people before. This is ironic, because, depending on your personality and temperament, this may be the time you *least* want to be around people. I get it. I'm a people person to the core, but even I felt like hiding in my bedroom twelve hours a day the first few days after my wife's death. But—and this is key—I was not alone. Outside my bedroom door, my brother and sister were working to take care of my needs. My pastors were always checking in on me and attending to my spiritual needs. My church family overwhelmed me with encouraging notes, texts, and emails—not to mention six weeks' worth of meals. I and everyone I have talked to about loss can attest to the fact that you need a community to fall back on during this time. So surround yourself with trusted support people and don't be afraid to ask for help.

Step ❹: Explore Music as Therapy

As I mentioned in chapter 3, I strongly encourage you to explore the soothing, healing power of music as you walk through this time. Music has a way of capturing the deepest longings of our heart and putting words to our most indescribable feelings. Instead of sitting in utter silence, put some background music on. Play songs that mean something to you and your loved one. If you're a person of faith, dive into the deep well of praise and worship songs. It is amazing how powerfully our minds attach memories to melodies. For example, my mother-in-law was moved into my home for the final stages of her hospice care. I learned so much just by watching my wife, Melyn, care for her mother, Helen. One night while we were around Helen's bedside, Melyn played some modern interpretations of classic hymns such as "How Great Thou Art" and "Amazing Grace." Though she had been in and out of lucidity all day, Helen's entire face lit up with recognition at the long-loved worship songs from her childhood. She came alive again in those moments. From that moment on, those songs will have a deeper meaning for my wife, Melyn, as well. Whenever she listens to them in the future, she'll remember this special moment she shared in her mother's final days. The music cemented the memories in her brain, and I know they're a big part of Melyn's healing journey.

Step ⑤: Get Off the Sofa

Even if you don't feel like moving off the sofa, get yourself up and do something physical. I found tremendous healing in my long morning walks and even in playing golf. Sometimes I found myself alone on the driving range channeling all my grief, frustration, and anger through my club and into that poor, unsuspecting little golf ball. If you normally work out, keep making time for the gym. If you enjoy exercising with friends every week, don't give it up during this season. There are many online options such as stretching, yoga, and low impact cardio workouts available if you are not ready to go out with a group. You aren't dishonoring your loved one by "playing"; rather, you're finding therapeutic relief in physical activity. Exercise gives you the physical stamina you need for the days ahead, and it literally floods your brain with feel-good chemicals. Yes, you may need medication to get through these weeks and months, but I encourage you to start with the best *natural* antidepressant: exercise.

Step ⑥: Be Honest about How You Feel

Be open and honest with yourself and others about how you're feeling and what you're experiencing. This is not the time to put on a brave face. So often we try to bury our feelings when we bury a loved one, but that never works. Those emotions *will* surface at some point and in some way. By facing them head-on, being transparent about your experience of grief, you can deal with them in a timely and healthy manner, rather than spring-loading them in a trap that snaps without warning later.

Step **7**: Share with Others

Sharing with others is an important part of being honest with yourself about how you're feeling. You can find tremendous comfort by expressing your pain and questions to trusted friends, mentors, pastors, or even in a grief group environment. You might also try connecting with others in our Survive-Alive-Thrive online community.

Step **8**: Celebrate Happy Memories

I encourage you to actively celebrate and discuss happy memories of times you shared with your loved one. This gives you the chance to relive some of your most precious memories, and it also invites others to share *their* memories of the person you've lost. This exchange of memories is a beautiful thing, and it's generally the reason people find themselves laughing through their tears at a memorial service or wake. In addition to sharing stories, you might find comfort in surrounding yourself with pictures of your loved one in happier times. I explained earlier that I removed many of the pictures around the house after Victoria's death, but certainly not all of them. I chose my favorite photos and placed them strategically throughout the house so I could interact with those specific memories on my terms. I didn't want to be surprised by a random photograph around every corner, but I did want to *see* Victoria around the house. Seeing her in happier times brought me peace. I just had to learn to give myself permission to enjoy the memories captured within the frame.

Step **9**: Show Grace to Others

Show grace to the people who are coming around you right now. They are most certainly going to do or say something stupid. People are well-intentioned and want to bring comfort, but most of us simply aren't equipped to communicate our love, concern, and desire to help. As a result, we misspeak, stumble, stammer, and say ridiculously inappropriate things. We *all* do—or we are all at least capable of it. So if you're walking the dark road right now, I encourage you to be patient with those around you. Show them the same grace you've received and give them the same love they're so desperately trying to give you.

Step ⑩: Access Online Resources

You will find many helpful online resources at www.SurviveAliveThrive. org. There, you can join an online grief group, read more about each season of healing, listen to dozens of other people share their stories of loss and healing, and much more. This is a safe way for you to dip your toes into a community without feeling any pressure to speak up or share your story. There will be plenty of time for that. So even if you need to stay incognito for a while, we'd love to have you.

Helping Others in Their Loss

Before we wrap up our discussion of Survive, I want to speak to those who may not have gone through a tremendous loss themselves but who are walking through this with someone who has. If your goal is to love and serve someone in their healing journey, please make a note of these practical dos and don'ts.

DO: Be Present

You'll show your love simply by showing up. Don't try to fill the silence and certainly do not offer trite words of comfort. Your loved one can't receive them right now, anyway. Just be there for them. Or to put it more bluntly, oftentimes the only two things you need to do are show up and be present.

DO: Be Proactive in Helping

If you really want to help someone, then *do something for them* instead of *asking them what you can do for them*. Take the initiative to buy them some groceries and leave them on their front porch. If their grass needs cutting, cut it. If their car is dirty, wash it for them. If they have young children, plan a play date and take the kids for the day. These don't have to be big deals. Just find something to do and do it.

DO: Stay in the Present When Talking

When connecting with someone who is in the Survive stage, it's important to stay in the active present. "What are you doing (right now)?" is much better than inquiring about their emotional state of mind. Further, if they are engaged in something you can help them with, it's an opportunity to act and provide support. If they're simply going for a walk, offer to go along and provide company.

DON'T: Say Insensitive Things

As my mother used to tell me as a young man, "Don't engage your mouth until your brain is in gear!" In that context, it is astounding how often we put both feet in our mouths when we're interacting with someone who's been through a terrible loss. We don't mean to. Our goal is to offer comfort and support. And yet, we can find ourselves saying something stupid and hurting the person we're trying to comfort. A woman who'd lost her young son told me about an encounter she had at the boy's funeral. Another woman put her arm around the grieving mother and said, "Look, you're young. You can have more children. In another year or two, you won't even remember this." When my friend burst out crying, the woman tried to backtrack and explain what she meant to say, but the damage was done.

Sometimes, even the simplest statement of support or question can go very wrong. Shortly after losing his wife, a friend explained, "The most insensitive thing someone can ask me is, 'Are you okay?' Because the answer is, no, I will never be okay with my wife's death. This is something I will walk with for the rest of my life...." He continued, "Am I okay? No. If I were *okay*, there'd be something wrong with me."

Now my friend was still very close to his wife's death at that time and has experienced much healing over the years since we had that initial discussion. But the point is that people in the Survive stage are more sensitive than they'll be at any other part in their healing journey. What you say to them will make a bigger impact than either of you realize, so it's advisable to be extremely careful with your words here.

DON'T: Put the Burden of Asking for Help on the Hurting Person

How many times have you either said or heard this phrase, "Let me know if there's anything I can do"? It's as though human beings are preprogrammed from birth to dribble that useless sentence out whenever someone we know is going through a difficult time. We mean well when we say it, but almost no one ever comes back to us and says, "Hey, you told me to let you know if you can do anything. So, here's what I need...."

The problem with that statement is that it puts the full burden of asking for help on the hurting person. Sure, we're making ourselves available, but we're still forcing the grieving person to ask us for a favor—and this is extremely difficult for most people, especially during times of intense grief and loss. As I've said, if you see a need, then take action and meet it without being asked. This is actually two gifts of grace in one: first, you took care of a need for the person, and second, you didn't force them to ask you for it.

DON'T: Offer to Help if You Won't Follow Through

This warning goes along with the previous one. If, by some miracle, the hurting person actually does think of something you can do for them after you offered to help, do not for any reason let them down. Please avoid the temptation to say, "Let me know if there's *anything* I can do," particularly if you aren't prepared to do *anything*. That's what you told them, right? That you'd do *anything*? If you put that offer on the table, you're obliged to follow through.

You can't imagine how difficult it is for someone in the initial shock after a loss to ask for a favor. When every instinct tells them to isolate, to shut themselves off from the world and mourn alone, it takes a miracle for them to not only think of something you can do but to also drum up the courage to actually *ask*. Turning them down at that point is a slap in their face.

I experienced this firsthand after my wife's death. A few weeks after Victoria's death, I had to catch a plane for a short trip. Normally, Victoria would have dropped me off at the airport, but she was gone. I remembered a friend had told me just a few days prior to let him know if I needed anything. "*Anything* you need," he said. "Just let me know." So, I did. I called this friend and asked if he could take me to the airport early the next morning for my 6:00 a.m. flight. "Oh wow, Mark," he stammered. "That's really early. I've been working a lot lately, and I'm really trying to prioritize my sleep. Could you ask someone else?"

I'm sure you're as disappointed in my friend's response as I was. But how easy would it be for you to do the same thing? We put these offers to help out there without thinking them through. I'm telling you, though, that you cannot pull the rug out from under someone going through the Survive stage so close to their loss. Their world has just been devastated. If you offer to help with *anything*, then be ready to help with *anything*.

Navigating through Devastation

Earlier, I described the onset of the Survive-Alive-Thrive journey as a series of ripples emanating from a central point of impact. It's easy to picture that like a stone hitting the surface of a pond. In actuality, however, it feels more like a bomb going off than a pebble hitting the water. That's how I experienced Victoria's death. For me, it wasn't a gentle drop in the pond; it was a bomb that fell into the middle of my life and took out everything in its immediate path. The first few days, weeks, and months were devastating. It was all I could do to simply survive the loss. My only goal was to make it through each day. Then, after a few months, I realized I was finally able to breathe again. Routines were getting back to normal (or falling into a *new* normal). My son started college. I went back to work. I started hanging out with friends again. People stopped walking on eggshells around me. That's when I realized I had made it through Survive, and now it was time to face Alive. That's where we're heading next.

Questions for Discussion

1. Describe the first two weeks following your "ground-zero moment." Include every decision you had to make, action you had to take, issue you had to research, person you had to meet with, arrangements you had to make, legal issue you had to deal with, and so on.

2. What was your biggest emotional response to your loss? What outward reactions/manifestations did that lead to? Be specific.

3. Reflect on your experience a day after ground zero, a week after, a month after, and so on. How did your experience and responses change over the first few months?

4. Most people use the word *shock* to describe their initial response to loss. Is this true for you? How did that shock present itself in your life?

5. Have you experienced any surprising or uncharacteristic emotional outbursts during the Survive stage? Explain.

6. Has a feeling of powerlessness characterized your loss experience? What more do you wish you could have done to make a positive impact in your situation?

7. How has your natural personality style impacted your experience throughout Survive? Has this affected how others view you and your loss experience?

8. In what ways has your backstory informed your experience of loss? What lessons, history, or experiences in your past shaped the way you reacted to your loss?

9. Has your faith/worldview been a comfort or a pain point as you work through your loss throughout Survive? Explain.

10. What has been the most helpful action step you've taken to work through your grief during the Survive stage? What's been the least helpful?

11. What have your friends and family members done to support you during Survive? What was especially helpful? What was accidentally hurtful?

Chapter 8

THE ALIVE STAGE

—

Part 1: Balancing on the High Wire

WHILE THE SURVIVE SEASON IS ALL ABOUT TRIAGE, THE ALIVE stage is more like a high-wire balancing act. You can imagine yourself walking the tightrope that bridges the gap between your old life and your new one. Behind you is the life you lived with your loved one, and ahead of you is the new life everyone keeps expecting you to embrace—something you're still not sure you can do. And, in the middle, there you are, slowly plodding along, one foot in front of the other, trying not to fall. It's like you're holding a circus performer's balancing pole, with your heart and soul healing on one end and all your practical responsibilities piled up on the other. It's all you can do to keep your balance, let alone make much forward progress. But on we go.

After Victoria died, my Survive stage was full of pain and challenges, but there was at least one thing that kept me sane: my "cocoon of protection." The people in my life came around me like guard dogs, protecting me and taking charge of things like planning meals, answering my phone and doorbell, getting groceries, and so on. And I was truly blessed to have had people near me who were ready to listen, talk, or weep with me. I hope and pray you have people who can or will do the same for you. But now, as the initial shock wears off and your loved ones return to their lives, you might find yourself unprotected. You're emerging from a time of great sorrow, and it's scary to realize you're losing some of your coverage. Whatever happened and whatever your loss, you're now realizing that you have to reengage with worldly responsibilities and make the choice to live again. It's time, once again, to try to act and feel like you're *alive*, ready or not.

Where You Are and What You're Facing

In this chapter, we're going to explore the Alive stage of the grief process and identify significant earmarks of this season and the unique nature of each of them. If you place yourself in the Alive stage, it is my hope these earmarks help you better understand where you are in the journey. As such, action steps related to this stage in the grieving process are proposed in the next chapter.

I will also review several of the most common challenges associated with the Alive stage, and what you can expect to encounter as you continue the healing process. The goal remains the same: to prepare you for what's ahead and to inform those who may be supporting someone they love through the journey of loss.

Finding Yourself in the Alive Stage

When I work through the Survive-Alive-Thrive model with others, people always want to know when Alive starts (or when it is *supposed* to start) and how long it lasts. I want to say right off the bat that there is no specific timeline that everyone follows. Some people will stay in Survive longer than others, while some are more naturally inclined to take a more "power-grieving" approach. There is no right time or wrong time. There is only *your* time, and that generally depends on your Personal  Blueprint—which I have defined as a goulash of your unique personality and temperament (introverted or extroverted, highly sensitive/expressive or emotionally guarded, action-oriented or methodical thinker, and so on) and your backstory (history of trauma, family of origin, relationships, and so forth).

In fact, you'll note that the stages of Survive-Alive-Thrive are interconnected on the model graphic. The space shared by the overlapping circles represent time spent coexisting in the adjacent stages. The transition within the grieving and healing process from Survive to Alive, for example, is subtle and you likely have or will experience emotional responses from each season at the same time or go back and forth from one to another throughout the transition phase. It is not a clean- or clear-cut graduation of linear accomplishment; rather, it's a gradual transition as your grieving process progresses over time.

As such, we don't knowingly choose or willfully push our way to move out of Survive and into Alive; in fact, we rarely even realize we're *in* Alive until we look up and notice a handful of key earmarks that our life and recovery have changed. What we were incapable of doing during Survive starts popping up in our day-to-day lives again, and we start to get a sense of what our *new normal* looks like. While I can't give a complete list of *every* earmark, there are three recurring ones I've noticed in most of the people I've interviewed.

ALIVE STAGE OVERVIEW	
HALLMARKS OF THE SEASON	WHAT THAT CAN MEAN/LOOK LIKE
1 MAKING TIME FOR EMOTIONAL HEALING	Aware of the need to process your grief
	New desire to talk to someone about your experience
2 PROACTIVELY SCHEDULING ACTIVITIES	Able to look past today's needs and plan for tomorrow
	Scheduling simple things like a dentist appointment
	Re-entering social activities
	New sense of relational normalcy with friends and family
	Return to church on a regular basis
3 RESUMING LIFE TASK DUTIES	Room in your life for *boring* things again
	Resume basic housework tasks

Hallmark 1: Making Time for Emotional Healing

In the initial aftermath of a loss, the best we can usually do is grit our teeth and focus on making it from one day to the next. That's why I call that stage *Survive*. Early on, you may have been given the opportunity to arrange for time with a pastor or person of your faith. Counseling may be available with social workers, psychologists, and other mental healthcare professionals. Some survivors I've talked to reported entering exploratory counseling before even having their loved one's funeral. If that feels right and talking with a pastor or counselor will bring you some peace and insight at that stage, I highly encourage doing so. Others chose to wait as they did not feel ready for a formal conversation with either. In my case, it was a mix. I was fortunate to have close relationships with several pastors who graciously came to my home and with whom I was able to share my heart and grief. I am very grateful to each for their acts of kindness. That said, it wasn't until I had returned from a healing getaway trip with my son eight weeks following Victoria's death before the thought of formal counseling even came on my radar.

However, as I reentered the world, I became acutely aware of my need for some professional help in processing my grief. Sure, I was just entering the Alive stage of my processing journey and still felt very, very raw emotionally, but I felt a strong desire to talk to someone about what I was feeling. That desire was new. Up to that point, I'd felt this indescribable pain and had no ability or inclination to articulate it. One day, however, I realized I really wanted to talk about it. It was a deep need, something I just had to do. That's what led me into several months of productive and healing counseling sessions with George, which I discussed in chapter 4. That intentional, proactive desire to address our own emotional healing is a clear sign that we've exited the Survive stage and have at least stepped into Alive. I'll talk more about counseling in the following chapter.

Hallmark **2**: Proactively Scheduling Activities

Survive is marked by reaction. It seems everything you do there is simply a reaction to something else. It's visceral, much like a wounded animal keeping a sharp eye on his surroundings and reacting accordingly to any perceived threats. As we enter Alive, though, we gradually shift out of that reactionary mindset and put some forethought into our lives and activities. We're not just focused on what must happen *today*; instead, we're able to look a day, a week, or a month down the road and make plans. Too often, when we lose someone, we shut down completely. We lock everything down and act as though we've lost our own lives as well. But scheduling something as simple as a dentist or counselor appointment is a testament to the fact that you are reclaiming your life. By committing to be at a certain place at a certain day and time, you are willfully envisioning yourself *being there*. Though it sounds simple, that's a huge step into Alive territory. You're proclaiming to the world through your calendar and commitments that you are still alive, that you still exist and are active in this world.

This is especially meaningful when it comes to making new social commitments. This shows that the social fog is lifting, that you're more than a burden to your friends and family members. Throughout Survive, they came around you to care for you, serve you, and keep you going during the darkest days of your life. Now, in Alive, they just want to hang out. They want to enjoy your company again, and you want to enjoy theirs. The relational dynamic is shifting back to normal, and there's a certain peace and comfort to that sense of relational normalcy. This doesn't mean you're ready to go to a big party or throw yourself headfirst into nightly social commitments—unless, of course, you have a naturally outgoing personality and that high degree of social activity feels natural and comfortable to you. If so, going out and being around friends every night may be exactly what you need.

However, if you're a more introverted, introspective, and/or private person, that level of commitment sounds like torture to you even on your best days. You certainly don't want that *now*. But you might be ready to meet a few close friends for lunch, go see a movie, and enjoy a cup of coffee with someone without feeling like they're taking care of you. You aren't fully reengaged in society yet, but the *process* of reengagement is well underway.

If you are part of a faith community, this is also when you start reappearing at church on a regular basis. The first few Sundays, your church family probably greeted you with hugs and awkward expressions of sympathy. Now, though, you've been reengaged for a little while and your loss isn't the first thing they think of when they see you. They greet you with a smile rather than a tear, and that goes a long way toward making life feel "normal" again.

Hallmark 3: Resuming Life Task Duties

Ironically, one of the most exciting earmarks that you're stepping into the Alive stage is that there's room in your life for *boring* things again. When you're in Survive, nothing is boring because everything's on fire. You spend all day, every day jumping from one crisis to the next, whether it's emotional, relational, financial, funeral-related, or a hundred other crises. You aren't as concerned about things such as shopping or cleaning the house because those things seem so unimportant. Besides, we often have people around us who are taking care of those things for us immediately following a big loss. As time goes on, however, we find ourselves picking up a duster or pushing a vacuum all on our own. We notice the pantry is bare, make a shopping list, and head to the store. We look at the hungry faces of our children at dinnertime and preheat the oven and thaw some chicken. It's all so . . . mundane—and yet it is a crucial landmark in our healing journey. It shows that our minds are shifting out of the shock-and-awe numbness of Survive and into the day-to-day reality of Alive.

Facing the Challenges of Alive

As you move into the Alive season, you'll find that life doesn't seem to care that you've already been through a horrible, painful loss. Going through one big loss doesn't inoculate us from future tragedy. So let's explore some of the common difficult situations you're likely to face during this season of recovery.

NOTABLE CHALLENGES OF THE ALIVE STAGE

NOTABLE CHALLENGES	WHAT THAT CAN MEAN/LOOK LIKE
1 ADDRESSING QUESTIONS ABOUT FAITH	Confusion over why God would allow pain and suffering
	Struggles with understanding death, grace, and eternal life
	Potential for an even stronger, closer relationship with God
2 GOING BACK TO WORK	Return to normal work schedule
	Boss is understanding but expects your work to be done
3 SETTLING ESTATE MATTERS	Fully engaged in paperwork to settle the loved one's estate
	Estate executors often blamed for the contents of the deceased's will
	Potential for family arguments over who gets what
4 FACING FINANCIAL MATTERS	Dealing with lost income if the deceased worked
	Fear as you get your arms around a new family budget
	Need for advice and guidance if family finances is new to you

NOTABLE CHALLENGES	WHAT THAT CAN MEAN/LOOK LIKE
5 FACING LOST LOVED ONE'S BELONGINGS	Deciding what to do with the deceased's personal items, clothes, etc.
	Being selective in what photos and mementos to leave around the house
	Finding "surprises" throughout the house
	Clearing out a deceased parent's entire houseful of memories
6 DEALING WITH "THE LOOK"	People want to ask how you're doing, which brings you back into your pain
	Friends accidentally make you feel damaged
7 IDENTITY CRISIS AND SOCIAL ADJUSTMENTS	Asking yourself, "Who am I without the person I lost?"
	Widow or widower not sure how *not* to be a wife or husband
	Parent suddenly removed from school activities after the death of a child
8 DATING AND NEW RELATIONSHIPS	Coming to terms with life as a single person after the death of a spouse
	Confusion over how to talk about your deceased spouse with future relationships
	Guilt over "moving on"

Challenge **1**: Addressing Questions about Faith

If you're a person of faith, it's easy to question why God allows us to experience such intense pain in our lives. Many people, in fact, use "the problem of pain" as an excuse to reject the very existence of a loving God.

While you may have clung to Him for dear life during the Survive stage, you may find yourself asking these important questions as you settle into Alive. One father who recently lost his twelve-year-old daughter to cancer remembers asking, "Why, God? ... What's going on? I mean, what can You possibly be trying to accomplish with this?"

This can obviously lead some people away from faith. However, the miraculous thing I've seen in hundreds of survivor stories is that this can also lead people into an even stronger, much more intimate relationship with God. Many people I spoke with were adamant that God gave them the strength to get through the ordeal. They also spoke of the many blessings God provided before, during, and after their loved one's death. I'll talk more about finding the blessings in loss and suffering in section 3 of this book.

Challenge ❷: Going Back to Work

At some point in the Survive stage, if you work outside the home, you had to go back to work—and it was probably before you were mentally prepared to return to the day-to-day grind. Oregon is the only state in the country that has any type of bereavement leave law, requiring companies with twenty-five or more employees to grant bereavement leave for the death of a family member—but even that is filled with caveats.[7] Hopefully, your employer showed grace early in the process. Your boss probably told you take it easy the first week or two, but that grace period eventually expires. While your leader may have left muffins and a sympathy card on your desk your first day back, before long, she just wants your spreadsheets and sales reports done on time.

---

7 "Oregon Bereavement Leave Law," *Employment Law Handbook*, Accessed June 25, 2020, https://www.employmentlawhandbook.com/leave-laws/state-leave-laws/oregon/bereavement-leave/.

Challenge ❸: Settling Estate Matters

As we saw in the Survive stage, it's shocking how much paperwork is involved in a loved one's death. Wills, death certificates, probate court, bank accounts, clearing debts, having the person declared legally dead, shutting off or changing the names on home utilities, selling property …what a nightmare. It's like you're suddenly dropped in the middle of a crazy combination CPA/MBA/law school exam with no preparation and the highest of stakes. Your personal financial stability and security may be on the line while you're struggling to understand out-of-date certificates, life insurance, and the tax implications of your loved one's death. For many, this high level of detail comes easily. For others, it's a complete mystery. If meticulous filing and organization is terrifying to you when you're having a *good* day, you certainly wouldn't want to be thrown into it right after going through the worst thing that's ever happened to you. And yet, that's what happens. We're all required to become financial planners and tax and accounting experts at a time when our brain is still half shut down.

This isn't just a financial and legal train wreck, either. We can't forget the myriad emotional traps that go along with estate issues. Families are torn apart after the death of a parent when, for example, siblings bicker over who gets what. Disgruntled family members crawl out of the woodwork to complain about being overlooked or, as they may claim, intentionally left out. Even when there is a clear, definitive will and estate plan to follow, there's always someone who gets their feelings hurt and points the finger at someone else. Executors are often blamed for the contents of the estate plan, and sometimes they're even accused of manipulating the deceased person's intentions prior to their death. It's a crazy, hurtful blame game that strikes when we're at our most vulnerable.

Challenge **4**: Handling Financial Matters

If the person you lost was a key financial provider for your family, you will no doubt experience a rush of fear as you sit down to work on your budget and pay your bills for the first year or so after he or she has passed. If you are in this situation, know that you are not alone and do not hesitate to reach out to friends and family for advice and support. Fear thrives in silence, so cut it off at the knees by asking for help. And if you're reading this and do not personally have life insurance or any plan in place to provide for your loved ones in your absence, make this a priority *today!* I've talked to hundreds of widows and widowers who were left not only mourning but terrified of how to make ends meet without their spouse. If you really love your loved ones, you won't leave them to drown in the fear of insecurity after you're gone. Get this done *now*.

Challenge **5**: Facing Your Lost Loved One's Belongings

Returning home from my two-week escape to Hawaii after Victoria's death was one of the hardest things I've ever done. As I said in chapter 4, I couldn't even park my car in the garage when we returned from the airport. The house—especially the garage—had too many memories waiting to pounce as soon as I walked in the door. Facing this issue by dealing with Victoria's belongings was a key milestone in my progression into the Alive stage.

I've talked to dozens of others who have had the same experience after losing a spouse. Grown men and women also have the same or similar experience when cleaning out their parents' home after their death. It's so hard to pack away someone's life into boxes and garbage bags, and there are always surprises. One woman I spoke with told me about finding dozens of bags of snack-size chocolate bars all through her mother's home after her passing. She found chocolate in the bedroom closet, in the nightstand, in the coffee table, and even under the bathroom sink! My friend never knew her mother did this.

If you're a parent who has lost a young child, you're faced with the question of what to do with your little one's bedroom. Do you leave it as he or she left it, making it a memorial to the child who once slept there? Is it okay to turn that room into an office or allow another child to move into it? When is it okay to do so? What do you do with the clothes, school supplies, trophies, spelling bee ribbons, and works of Crayola art? What's the *right* thing to do in that situation?

Clearly, addressing your loved one's belongings is a daunting task, but it's a clear sign you're moving into the Alive season. Even through the pain, you're identifying a need and making yourself deal with your new reality.

Challenge ⑥: Dealing with "the Look"

People who have been through a big loss know what I mean when I talk about "the look." It can seem that every time you run into someone you haven't seen in a while, they tilt their head, flash a little frown, and, as if talking to a wounded puppy, ask, "So, how *are* you doing? Are you *okay*? How are you *really?*"

One recent widow I interviewed described "the look" as a double-edged sword. No matter how good a day you were having before, this question drags you right back into your grief. You might get angry at them for bringing you back down, but then you feel guilty about your anger because, after all, they were just trying to show you compassion.

This hit me a couple of months after Victoria died. I'd been busy that summer doing all the legal things around her death, cleaning out the house, getting Andersen to college, and basically trying to keep my sanity. After weeks of dealing with all that, I was really looking forward to hanging out with a group of friends I hadn't seen in a while. We met at a steakhouse and had a fantastic time. Just being around a group of guys, laughing and talking like we always had, made me feel more alive and "normal" than anything else had that summer. It was the best time I'd had in a long, long time. But then, at the end of the night, these well-meaning friends did something that changed the entire *feel* of the night: they tried to pay for my dinner. Now, I know that seems like a small thing, but I'd been having steak nights with these guys for years. We *always* split the check; it was never even a question. So when they went to cover me, I was genuinely confused.

My buddies looked at one another and then said, "We've got your dinner, Negley."

"What do you mean, you've got my dinner?" I asked. "I got my share."

"Well," one of them offered, "we're just glad you could make it tonight. We've all been thinking about you. Buying you a steak is the least we can do."

Okay. I know my buddies meant well. I know they love me, and they were just trying to show me a simple act of kindness. But I've got to be honest: this *really* threw me off. They were treating me like I was broken. In a flash, I went from being a guy out with his buddies to a lonely widower who was just lucky enough to be out of his empty house for the night. That's not what I wanted or needed that evening. Instead of giving me the chance to move *through* my grief, acts like this just forced me back *into* my grief. We talked about it on the spot as close friends do, and they wanted to know if they *couldn't* buy me dinner then what *could* they do? "You're doing it," I said. "Just simply *being here* means the world to me." And it did.

Challenge 7: Identity Crisis and Social Adjustments

Another emotional response to loss in the Alive stage is a general sense of confusion about who we are without the person we've lost. One recent widower I talked to who had been married for nearly forty years described a total loss of identity because he didn't know how to be anything other than his wife's husband. A mother who'd recently lost her young child had a similar experience when she suddenly realized she was no longer a PTA mom. Whether a loss leaves us a widow/ widower, unexpectedly childless, a single parent, or even "orphaned" in our fifties, we all face a change in our sense of self. The "who am I?" question hangs in the air, and it often takes us months or years to figure out the answer.

In my case, Victoria and I were married with a son. We had been involved in several community organizations including sports teams, social clubs, and the like. We attended two couples' community groups through our church and had many good friends through those networks. However, I'd been "Victoria's husband" for a long time and navigating what it meant to be myself—*just me*—in relation to these groups and other people was difficult following her death. Those who knew us as a couple now saw me as *half* of a couple. The couple's groups kindly encouraged me to continue attending, but it was awkward and a reminder that my wife was no longer with me in this world. I realized I had to find different ways of connecting with the individuals within the previously defined *couples' friendships* that I valued. It also meant finding new social sets that were combinations of couples, singles, and others in transition.

Challenge **8**: Dating and New Relationships

A big part of the human experience is engaging other people in relationships. That certainly doesn't stop after you've gone through loss. Rather, it can get much *more* complicated. Your heart will tell you when you're ready to explore a potential romantic relationship, but if you think the dating scene is tricky in your twenties, imagine what it's like in your fifties after spending thirty years loving one person. At the same time, staying at home is also not the answer, as loneliness and isolation are tough on most of us. Many people prefer to start out with platonic and strictly friends' activities, which is a great way to reengage.

If you've lost a spouse, you may not feel like you would ever even want to love again. I certainly understand that. Whether that holds true or not, you still have plenty of living to do—and living in the world means building and engaging in relationships with other people ... even if it feels awkward.

Choosing to Live

I recently spent an afternoon with a widow who had lost her spouse a few years prior to our discussion. Her husband died tragically after falling off the roof while taking down their home's Christmas lights. It was a traumatic way to end what was their last holiday together, but after engaging in the grieving process, she had determined that she had reached the time to pick up the pieces of her life and move forward. "Just because someone you love dies," she said, "does not mean you have to die too."

My friend did what I've done, what countless others have done before us, and what you will do when the time is right: she *chose* to live again. You are still here. Yes, your life is different, but your life is not over. Engaging in the Alive stage is both a choice you make and an action you take. While your loss was *something that happened to you*, your healing journey will be *something you do*. And it won't happen by accident.

So, how do we practically take action in the Alive stage, and what emotional responses and outward reactions/manifestations can we expect? We'll explore this and more in the following chapter as we continue our discussion of Alive.

Questions for Discussion

1. I describe my support system during Survive as a "cocoon of protection" that receded as I moved into Alive. Did you have a similar experience? Discuss the adjustments you had to make as your family and friends returned to their own lives.

2. What earmark has most characterized your entry into Alive? If you aren't quite there yet, what changes or earmarks do you expect as you take the first steps out of the Survive stage?

3. Have you sought professional counseling to help you navigate your journey through this loss? If so, how has it been helpful? If not, what are your reservations about getting help?

4. How did it feel to resume "normal" activities? What fears and anxieties did you have as you stepped back into life?

5. Have you noticed a shift in the way your friends act around you now that you're further away from your initial point of loss? Explain.

6. What was the most intimidating challenge you faced as you moved into Alive?

7. If you were responsible for settling a deceased loved one's estate, explain that process. What do you wish you'd have known about the process earlier? What advice would you give others as they face this intimidating responsibility?

8. Describe your response to what one widow described in this chapter as "the look" other people give you. How does "the look" make you feel? What do you wish people would do instead?

9. Have you struggled with a loss of identity in the wake of your loss? Explain.

10. If you're a person of faith, what has your experience of loss taught you about God? Has this caused you to question your beliefs?

Chapter 9

THE ALIVE STAGE

Part 2: Emotional Elbow Room

*I*N SURVIVE, YOUR EMOTIONAL RESPONSES, OUTWARD REACTIONS/ manifestations, backstory, faith/worldview, life responsibilities, type of loss, and more were all swirling around under incredible pressure in the smallest circle of the Survive-Alive-Thrive model. Like shaking ten ping-pong balls in a goldfish bowl, collisions were rampant, leading to potentially cataclysmic emotional, mental, physical, and relational explosions. As you move into the Alive stage, in view of the emotional elbow room you've gained, things are spread out a bit more. Despite the incremental operating space, you still have a world of things spinning atomically as a result of your loss. You're surrounded by and engaging new responsibilities and difficulties, you're still dealing with the emotions and outward manifestations you developed during Survive, and now you're adding even more emotional responses to the mix. While the Alive stage gives you more breathing room, you should still expect "atomic" emotional collisions.

What to Expect in This Chapter

In this chapter, we're going to explore how our emotional reactions have changed now that we've transitioned to the Alive stage of our grief journey. While our Personal Blueprint influences our emotional responses and experiences in each stage of the grief process, in Alive, we'll see differences in how we can respond to the loss experience once we're balancing both life tasks and our healing process.

Importantly, I have sorted the emotional responses listed in this section into two categories: challenging and healthy. Regardless of which emotional responses you are currently experiencing or have experienced, this is not a test or contest. The goal simply remains to identify with your own personal experience and to embrace the idea that you are not alone in what you're going through. While we do not necessarily experience *all* of the responses listed, nor do we need to, there are likely those provided to which you can relate.

As in chapter 7, I will provide strategies and healthy steps to empower you to process and manage your grief on this next step on the path to hope and healing. Again, these suggestions are taken from my own personal experiences, from talking with and interviewing others who experienced loss, and from input from pastors and mental healthcare professionals. It's my hope and prayer that you will find ideas that can help you as you progress through the Alive stage and continue the healing process.

Emotional Responses to Loss: Alive Stage

It's impossible to anticipate every emotional response you'll face during this season of reengaging life after loss, but I do want to highlight several of the big issues I've seen in my own life and in the lives of those I've interviewed. I'll do this by breaking several of these responses into two categories: *challenging* and *positive*.

ALIVE STAGE: EMOTIONAL RESPONSES SNAPSHOT

CHALLENGING RESPONSES	WHAT THAT CAN MEAN/LOOK LIKE
1 FEELING OVERWHELMED	Overwhelmed by a flood of raw emotions, responsibilities, and tasks Sense that your whole world is out of control
2 SORROW, SADNESS, AND DESPAIR	Feeling of shock gives way to deep feelings of pain and sorrow Sense of despair settles in
3 FEELING THE PERSON'S ABSENCE	Sense of a missing piece in your life Accutely aware of the absence of the person you lost
4 ABSENTMINDEDNESS	Muddled thinking General forgetfulness, missed appointments, unpaid bills, and so forth
5 MOVING ON VS. HANGING ON	Desire to stay in your grief simply to feel the presence of your lost loved one Lessening pain may make you fear you're "forgetting" the person you lost Realization that you can only take so much pain Need for intentionality in giving yourself time to mourn
6 LONELINESS	Afraid to come home to an empty house Feeling of emptiness Not sure what to do with your free time

CHALLENGING RESPONSES	WHAT THAT CAN MEAN/LOOK LIKE
7 **ABANDONMENT**	Surprised by a sense (and possibly anger) that your loved one *left you*
	Adults often feel oddly *orphaned* by the death of their parents
8 **HYPERSENSITIVITY**	Intense, surprising emotional reactions sparked by photos or memories
	Friends may become skittish about mentioning your lost loved one
	General sense of awkwardness around the topic of the deceased

Challenging Response **1**: Feeling Overwhelmed

The first sensation, to which we've alluded several times, is a general sense of feeling overwhelmed by the flood of raw emotions, responsibilities, tasks, and concerns of life without your loved one. This is the Atomic Nature of Healing model in a nutshell: everything in your life can feel like it is spinning wildly out of control, and the mere thought of it is enough to make you want to crawl up in a little ball and hide under the covers. I've been there. This response makes sense for a little while as you take the initial impact of your loss. In Alive, however, you're forced out from hiding and begin tackling some of the tasks you could not handle during the Survive stage. That can be—and almost always is—immensely over-whelming. No matter how strong you think you are, taking those first few steps out into a scary new world takes time . . . and courage.

Challenging Response **2**: Sorrow, Sadness, and Despair

Sorrow, sadness, and despair are also common emotional responses at this stage. The leading reaction in Survive was shock; now, that shock has subsided, and we're left with the bitter reality of our loss. That's when these deep feelings of pain and emptiness settle in like a fog that rolls in after a storm. The thunder and lightning are gone, and all that's left are the clouds that obscure a life that was once so familiar yet now seems so foreign and scary. I believe this is why we begin to recognize our need for counseling during the Alive stage—because we want to grow past this despair as quickly as possible and talking about these dark feelings is the only thing we can think of to do that.

Challenging Response ❸: Feeling the Person's Absence

Along with the general feeling of sadness comes a specific sense that someone is missing from our lives. We all know what it's like to have a person-shaped hole in our lives, don't we? When we lose someone, our lives can feel like a puzzle that's one piece short. We're still here, still ourselves, but it's clear someone or something that was once a part of us has been removed, and that missing piece changes the overall look and feel of our lives.

Challenging Response ❹: Absentmindedness

Another likely emotional response is basic absentmindedness. One afternoon a few days after my wife's death, when I was still in a Survive-level state of shock, Andersen and I were running errands when I stopped for gas. When I finished and drove off, I heard a loud and violent *clang* behind me and realized I had driven off with the gas nozzle still attached to my car. Fortunately, these nozzles are made to break away easily without damaging the actual gas pump. I say *fortunately* because I did the same thing two days later. That's right: I drove off with the nozzle still attached to my car two times in three days! My son thought I'd lost my mind. He was probably right.

Flash forward a few months later when I was transitioning into the Alive stage. It had been a while since my incidents at the gas pumps, and my head was feeling much clearer. I still wasn't *all there*, though. One month, I forgot to pay my credit card bill. The customer service agent was happy to help me out and show me grace, but it later dawned on me how different my absentmindedness had become over those few months. I went from breaking gas pumps to overlooking bills without a second thought. Things were still hazy, but the mental mishaps weren't nearly as severe as they'd been earlier in the process.

Challenging Response **5**: Moving On vs. Hanging On

A surprising, counterintuitive response I personally felt after the death of my wife, and one that I've heard many other people discuss, is a strange conflict between the desire to *move on* from our mourning and the desire to *prolong* our mourning. In times of great grief, we can feel the presence of our loved one in a profound and powerful way. Even though our hearts are wracked with pain at their loss, we can still feel them in our anguish. Their presence settles over us like a warm blanket as we mourn. In those times, moving on feels impossible, but at the same time, we don't *want* to move on, because at least we can still feel the person with such intensity and intimacy.

When the grief is less extreme, we aren't hurting as much, but we also don't feel the person's presence as much. Sometimes, this can scare us, and we may fear we're already starting to forget the person—how they looked and smelled, how their voice sounded, what their laugh was like, how their arms felt wrapped around us. We naturally miss these things and never want to forget, so we toggle back into a period of intense grief just so we can experience the person again in the full, raw power of our mourning.

I found myself going back and forth, moving in and out of these episodes of mourning, as I journeyed through the Alive season. It was always nice to feel Victoria's presence, but ultimately, a human being can only take so much pain and heartache. You reach a point where finding relief from that pain is equally refreshing and empowering. This conflict between feeling a connection to your lost loved one by mourning and feeling some relief from your pain through emotional distancing can be quite a shock to those of us who are more inclined to power through our grief. You might assume "progress" means getting past these intense episodes of grief, but, at the same time, you sometimes find yourself wanting to experience them.

As a Christian, I have experienced the same concept through the deep and direct connection I felt with God in times of deep sorrow. There were times in my darkest days when I felt closer to God than ever, as He held me in His arms and wiped away my tears. Feeling His loving-kindness in those moments was intensely wonderful—if any part of that season could be described as *wonderful*. Later, when my grief was not so overwhelming, I found a surprising longing in my heart to experience that reconnection and life-giving tether to God that I had only experienced when I was so utterly dependent on Him.

To be clear, navigating the Alive season doesn't necessarily mean *moving on* or *hanging on*. Again, there's no right or wrong grief timeline within reasonable parameters. My only advice for those struggling with the conflict is to be honest with and true to yourself. If you need to grieve for a few hours, then grab a box of tissues, put your phone on "do not disturb," lock yourself in your bedroom, and go for it. There's no shame, and it won't cause you to regress in your healing journey. Rather, spending some time embracing your pain—not to mention the intense emotional presence of your loved one—can be exactly what you need to take the next step forward. My only caution here is not to spend *every* day like this; it's a *balance* of healthy progression. Again, your heart can only take so much. I encourage you to embrace these experiences, but then get up, dry your eyes, and go back out to face the world with a renewed sense of purpose and with your heart and mind reenergized from mourning the loved one you have lost.

Challenging Response **6**: Loneliness

The most common emotional response people feel as they move into Alive is a new sense of loneliness. It can obviously be experienced when losing a spouse, but it's also common when losing a parent, sibling, or child whose passing has left a hole in your heart. Life is different, and you'll feel that difference in various ways and at often surprising times. I've talked to many recent widows and widowers, for instance, who intentionally went out with friends every night for months simply because they dreaded going home to an empty house.

Loneliness is a monster we all fear. God made us to be relational beings, and when a loving relationship is ripped from our lives, it leaves us feeling empty and alone. We'll go to great lengths to avoid that pain and feeling of isolation.

Challenging Response **7**: Abandonment

When the person we love isn't there for us anymore, it's not uncommon to feel a sense of abandonment—often followed by a sting of guilt. We're ashamed to admit that we feel our loved one *left us*, but that's exactly how I felt every morning when I woke up and saw the other half of the bed completely undisturbed. I'd gotten so used to seeing either Victoria asleep or seeing her crumpled sheet and discarded blanket beside me. It was literally the first thing I saw most days for decades, but now there was no trace of her each morning. And, honestly, it felt like I had been left there all alone.

While this response is perhaps most obvious in the case of losing a spouse, it certainly isn't exclusive to widows and widowers. Adults, for example, are often surprised to discover a new sense of childlike abandonment after the death of one or both parents. I was in my forties when my mother died, and I've heard many others describe this as feeling "orphaned" in their fifties or sixties. We're never too old—or prepared— to feel the hurt of losing the mother who kissed our scraped knees or the father who made us feel safe at night.

Challenging Response **8**: Hypersensitivity

A common emotional response to loss that still manages to catch us by surprise is a powerful, sometimes crippling hypersensitivity to things that remind us of the person we've lost. It's not unusual for us to be interrupted in the middle of a wonderful, happy day with a crying spell after seeing a picture or hearing a comment that reminds us of our loved one. Even something as innocuous as a friend asking how we're doing can send us into an emotional spiral, as the full weight of our loss comes crashing down on us seemingly out of nowhere. This can lead to many awkward encounters with well-meaning friends and loved ones and can leave them scratching their heads wondering what they did wrong.

Our friends and family members can also become hypersensitive around us out of fear of saying or doing something wrong and thereby hurting our feelings. While I respect their concern, no one wants to feel like everyone around them is walking on eggshells. For example, a few months after my wife took her life, I was enjoying an afternoon on the golf course with a few close friends. One buddy—who's always had a flare for the dramatic—was frustrated with his game after several bad shots. Lining up his putt on the green just a few feet from the hole, he loudly declared, "If I don't make this shot, I'm going to kill myself!"

Our group (including me) laughed at his outburst, but then a look of panic shot across his face. He looked up at me and said, "Oh, Mark! I am *so sorry!* I can't believe I said that." It created an awkward moment for all of us, and I felt like I had to relieve the tension for everyone. I laughed it off and assured him I understood what he meant and how he meant it. But it was a clear reminder that *everyone* is prone to hypersensitivity after a big loss.

Common Positive Emotional Responses

While the loneliness, sensitivity, and fear responses above are quite common, the Alive stage can also include positive experiences, emotional breakthroughs, and personal growth. This is the time when you're learning how to live again, when you're figuring out how to honor the person you've lost while still working toward a rich, full, and productive life without him or her. This creates a million little victories along the way, whether it's getting home from a night out with friends and realizing that you truly had fun or simply enjoying a quiet evening at home alone without descending into a fit of tears. These little wins add to an emerging sense that you'll get through this difficult time and come out the other end victorious.

ALIVE STAGE: EMOTIONAL RESPONSES SNAPSHOT	
POSITIVE RESPONSES	**WHAT THAT CAN MEAN/LOOK LIKE**
① CLOSER RELATIONSHIPS	Opportunities to dive deeper into existing relationships
	Exploring new relationships as an *individual* rather than as part of a couple
② GRATITUDE AND APPRECIATION	Chance to see others' lovingkindness in the wake of your loss
	Appreciative of the investment your friends and family poured into you
	Ability to see blessings in your loss experience
③ RE-ENERGIZED FAITH	Unprecedented opportunities to see God work in your life
	Stirred out of a "lazy" faith and into an active relationship with God

Positive Response ①: Closer Relationships

One common healthy response is a new or renewed sense of closeness in your existing relationships. When in the Alive stage, many of us experience enhanced and deeper bonds among family members and friends. If you've lost a spouse to death or divorce, this is an opportunity to engage with other people *on your own*, rather than as part of a couple. This can lead to stronger, much more personal one-on-one relationships with the people you already know and love. Plus, their care and attention during your healing journey may show you a whole new side to them as well. It's not uncommon for mere acquaintances to become best friends during this season, as you have the chance to engage with and see the loving-kindness of people who may have only been on your periphery before your loss.

Positive Response **2**: Gratitude and Appreciation

Likewise, feelings of gratitude and appreciation are common healthy responses after a loss. As we go through the Survive and Alive stages, we are blessed to witness the very best our friends and family have to offer. Their love, support, attention, and acts of kindness often mean the difference between healing and struggling for those of us recovering from a loss. I can't imagine going through the tragedies in my life without such a wonderful group of men and women, and I could not be more thankful for the care they gave me when I needed it most. No matter how dark and selfish the world seems to be at times, a season of loss seems to bring everyone to their senses and can call us to act and embrace others in a loving sense of community.

Positive Response **3**: Reenergized Faith

There are a handful of other healthy responses that are common among people of faith during the Alive stage. First and foremost, our gradual journey into our new lives gives us unprecedented opportunities to see God work and get to know Him on an entirely new level. Oftentimes, faith feels lazy when our lives are going well. It's like my friend Steve told me at the start of my friendship with God in 1999: "Happy and successful people who are enjoying life rarely start looking to God for answers unless something goes wrong." Steve could not have known how prophetic his words were at the time. I am deeply grateful that his words swayed my heart back then, because in the years following that discussion in my back yard, I've been through an unbelievable amount of hardship and loss. In retrospect,

Steve's comment—"unless something goes wrong"—was clearly an understatement in my case.

Of course, the good news is that when things did go wrong—when all seemed lost and I had nothing left to give physically, mentally, emotionally, or spiritually—I was blessed to have experienced God stepping in and revealing Himself in amazing new ways. That sense of companionship means *everything* to many of us in times of heartache. When I had nowhere else to go, no one else to turn to, no other hope for the strength to make it through, I fell on my face before God. And, in those early-morning walks in the park, Jesus picked me up and pointed me in the right direction. He hasn't left my side since.

Suggested Step for Healing Progression

While Survive is about *saving* your life, Alive is about *living* your life. Or I guess we should say, it's about *reengaging* our lives following loss. How do we do that? The following list offers some healthy steps that will get you started and help you continue your healing journey.

HEALTHY STEPS: NAVIGATING THE *ALIVE* STAGE	
HEALTHY STEPS	WHAT THAT CAN MEAN/LOOK LIKE
1 LEAN ON YOUR FAITH	As the shock of loss wears off, it's easy to get lazy about your faith again
	Prayer is still important but doesn't feel as *urgent* as it did in Survive

HEALTHY STEPS	WHAT THAT CAN MEAN/LOOK LIKE
2 COUNSELING IS CRITICAL	Everyone needs *some* counseling after a significant loss event
	Goal is to access the core root of your emotional responses
	Impossible to self-diagnose every issue at this stage
	Counseling comes with many challenges that must be overcome
3 BE HONEST ABOUT YOUR EMOTIONS	Many people are ashamed of what they're feeling
	Bottled-up emotions can poison you from the inside-out
	Powerful healing in giving voice to the pain of your heart
4 TAKE CARE OF YOUR BODY	Exercise can help unblock "stopped up" emotions
	Physical activity releases feel-good chemicals in your brain
	Avoid "emotional eating"
5 GO OUTSIDE	"Vitamin Sunshine" helps bring new life to a broken heart
6 HELP SOMEONE ELSE	Gives you a chance to stay busy while also improving someone's life
	Provides anonymity, meaning no one at a soup kitchen will ask about your loss

HEALTHY STEPS	WHAT THAT CAN MEAN/LOOK LIKE
7 ACCEPT AND ASK FOR HELP	Different needs than in Survive, but you still need help
	People *want* to help you on your journey
	You may need help with things like budgeting, home repairs, lawn care, etc.
8 BEWARE OF NEGATIVE COPING MECHANISMS	Tempted to medicate your pain through alcohol, spending, avoidance, etc.
	Distractions are fine, but you can't heal by living a life full of distractions

Step **1**: Lean on Your Faith

For people of faith in the Alive stage, the most important thing to do is to learn to rely fully on God's companionship, love, and mercy in every part of your life. That might sound like a trite, "churchy" thing to say, but I could not be more serious or thoughtful in this recommendation.

People entering Alive often make two common mistakes:

- **They rely on God less.** We rely on God almost on instinct during the Survive stage because we literally can do nothing else. Unable to function beyond the bare minimum, we're forced to rely on God to see us through the darkest days. But then, as things level out and we move into Alive, our need for God is the same but our reliance on Him can start to fade. The more we're able to think, work, and function on our own, the less we're inclined to fully lean on Him. We may start to go back to our old ways of relying on ourselves—our own strength and power and intellect. This, I believe, is a costly mistake.

- **They stop praying.** Prayer is just as important in Alive as it was in Survive, but it doesn't feel as desperate and urgent. We need answers during the Survive stage largely because our brains can't function, so we cry out to God. Well, we need those answers just as much during the Alive stage, but the decreased desperation keeps us from crying out with the same intensity and regularity. Hear me on this: Prayer is simply talking to God as a friend and Father. Conversing with Him is a gift and privilege. We get to have personal, one-on-one conversations with the Creator of the universe! He's never too busy to talk. He's always there, always ready, always wanting to connect with each one of us.

Whether you're in Survive, Alive, Thrive, or anywhere in between, you need to seek God's heart and will on your journey. You never need Him *more* or *less* at any point; you simply *need Him*—always.

Step ❷: Counseling Is Critical

Hands down, the single most important thing I can recommend at this stage is getting quality counseling. Nothing was as powerful to me in my own recovery as the hours I spent talking with my counselor, George. He had insights and suggestions I never would have considered otherwise, and those sessions made it possible for me to progress through the grief journey and pursue the full and blessed life I now have all these years later. I don't care if you're a man or woman, young or old, introverted or extroverted, highly emotional or deeply introspective, rich or poor, married or single or widowed. If you are a *human* who has been through a significant loss, you need and will benefit from at least a little counseling.

Counseling at this stage is about accessing the core root of the emotional responses you're experiencing and identifying whether the emotional responses are healthy or unhealthy and have a basis in fact or are unreasonable. These things can be impossible to self-diagnose when your heart and mind have been through the wringer of a tragic loss.

Counseling Challenges

Though essential, it's fair to say that counseling comes with a laundry list of challenges, such as:

1. **It's expensive.** Many families simply can't afford weekly hour-long sessions at $125 each. In many cases, even if you *can* afford the expense, it can be difficult to schedule meetings that work around your schedule and the counselor's.

2. **Insurance is complicated.** In fact, insurance is often little to no help in these situations, as the insurance companies put ridiculous restrictions on mental healthcare and most counselors are so frustrated by the red tape that they refuse to take any forms of insurance anyway. At most, many counselors will give you receipts for each session formatted in a way that allows you to turn it in to insurance yourself. But that only adds to your paperwork burden during an already stressful and busy time in your life.

3. **It takes a lot of time.** Many people are surprised to discover the time investment for counseling. Some assume it's like taking their car in for service, thinking one or two sessions is all it takes to "get fixed." That is simply not true. Most counseling journeys involve weekly or twice-weekly sessions at the beginning, eventually reducing to bi-weekly sessions and then maybe one counseling "check in" per month until they are finally released after *months* of intense counseling work. Finding the time to undertake this crucial journey can be just as much of a headache as finding the money to pay for it.

   While I recommend counseling for everyone who's gone through a life-changing loss, I know these challenges can seem insurmountable. If nothing else, though, I encourage you to at least ask your local church about any free counseling services they or other ministries in the area provide. This is a huge need, and most churches have *some* accommodations for it.

4. **Finding the Right Counselor.** Finding the right counselor for you may take time, and I recommend you have introductory sessions with a few

different counselors before committing to one. Think of it as the start of a new relationship—because it is. Your counselor will come to know you better than most of your friends, so make sure you're comfortable with him or her. Some things you should consider as you look include:

- Are you interested in a secular counselor or a Christian counselor? Their technical approaches may be similar, but a Christian counselor will have a personal connection and appreciation for how your worldview is impacting your journey as a person of faith. Just be sure your counselor has all the necessary education and training in counseling. You aren't seeing them *merely* for spiritual encouragement; you need them to help you process your emotions, and that requires specific training.
- What counseling methodology are you most interested in? As you explore counselor options, you'll find that they each have specialized training in different types of counseling. Take the time to understand those options so you know what to expect and can make the decision you'd be most comfortable with
- Seek advice from trusted resources while making your decision and try to talk with someone who has firsthand knowledge of the person you're considering.
- How much time are you willing and/or able to commit to counseling?
- Would you be more comfortable with a male or female counselor?
- Is your counselor available after hours?
- Does the counselor offer in-person sessions, online/video conferencing sessions, or both?

Whoever you choose and whatever method they use, expect counseling to be challenging and sometimes emotionally painful. That said, the investment has the potential to lead you into your healthy new life. In a way, you might think of counseling in terms of your grandmother's cod liver oil for your soul. It may not taste great, but it's working to improve your health.

So when it comes to counseling, my bottom line is this: Yes, it can be difficult—but it's too important to ignore. If there is any way you can find the time and money to care for your emotional and mental health in this way, do it. Prioritize this above nearly everything else. Remember, your loved one may be gone, but you'll have to live with *yourself* for the rest of your life. You want to make that relationship with yourself as healthy and enjoyable as possible.

Step 3: Be Honest about Your Emotions

Many of us act like we're scared or ashamed of our emotions, so we try to hide them behind a wall of armor. This is another area where personality styles and temperaments come into play. Some think showing their pain reveals a weakness. Others think the best thing to do is to maintain "a stiff upper lip" and "never let 'em see you sweat." Wrong, wrong, wrong.

There's a saying in alcohol and drug recovery: you're only as sick as your secrets. When we keep our emotions bottled up, they tend to poison us from the inside-out. It's only when we let them out, when we face them head-on that we're able to properly honor them, address them, and learn to grow through the pain we're feeling. Whether you're in deep mourning, angry, guilty, lonely, resentful, or anything else, be honest about what you're feeling. And then take it to the next step, which is to share it with someone else.

There is a powerful healing that takes place when we open up and share our pain with others. Of course, you may not be ready (yet) to speak up at a grief group, but that doesn't mean you can't find help in one. I've led many grief groups, and I'm always impressed by the people who show up week after week just to listen. I can tell their emotions are still too raw to fully articulate, but they still come to hear others' stories and offer support when and how they can. After a while, their trust increases and they see the value others experience in sharing, and they start opening up. It may just be with one or two close friends, but that little opening is all it takes. It's like slowly opening a release valve to let out some pressure.

Sharing our emotional journey is the whole point behind the online Survive-Alive-Thrive community. If you aren't even ready to sit in the back row of a grief group, then I encourage you to join our online community even if you don't post anything or share your story. Lurkers are welcome! As you browse the site or listen to the podcasts, you'll hear story after story of men and women who have been through exactly what you're going through now. By hearing others share their journey from loss to hope to happiness, I pray you'll at least catch a glimpse of where your story is going.

Step 4: Take Care of Your Body

While grief recovery is mostly about caring for our emotional and mental health, we can't let our bodies fall apart either. My walks in the park became runs and were a crucial step in my healing journey, not just because I needed a workout, but because I found tremendous emotional and mental release by being physically active. Our pain often makes us emotionally paralyzed; we're literally stopped up with clogged emotions. For many, exercise is critical to release emotional blockage and start moving forward again.

This doesn't mean you have to become a bodybuilder or commit to a daily sixty-minute workout regimen. Do a few push-ups or sit-ups. Try five minutes of stretching, deep breathing, or yoga poses to relax and quiet your mind (there are thousands of free videos on YouTube you can follow). Take a daily thirty- to sixty-minute walk in a park or your neighborhood. Just do *something* to get your heart rate up, and you'll experience a flood of feel-good chemicals in your brain that'll help you process everything else in your life.

And speaking of your body, be careful about what you're eating during this season of life. It can be easy for us to become emotional eaters during our grief recovery, soothing our broken hearts with a nightly package of chocolate chip cookies. That may feel good in the moment, but it's only causing more problems down the road. Grief may want you balled up on the sofa with a bag of potato chips twenty-four hours a day, but that's not where you'll find healing.

Step 5: Go Outside

The world outside is a beautiful, miraculous place that's literally teeming with life. Get out there and experience it. Even if you can only go as far as your front porch, make yourself sit out there for an extended stretch of time every day. Put a rocking chair on your patio or take a stroll to a local park with a folding chair and simply sit peacefully. If you're already back at work, try taking your lunch break outside. There's something about being outside in the "vitamin sunshine" that brings new life to a broken heart.

Step 6: Help Someone Else

This may seem impossible to you right now, but I encourage you to explore ways to serve other people at this stage of your recovery. Others may have given you so much to date that it will feel wonderful to give the gift of service to someone else now. Besides, serving brings with it an opportunity for anonymity, which may be exactly what you need right now. When you're serving meals to needy people at the local soup kitchen or women's shelter, they don't know you. They don't know what you've been through, they won't give you "the look," and they won't ask you how you're doing. All they feel is gratitude that you care enough to be there helping them. I've talked to dozens of people who started serving during their grief recovery and found a whole new passion that's fueled them for years afterward. You just might find that the best way to help yourself is to help someone else.

Step **7**: Accept and Ask for Help

On the topic of service, I want to encourage you to accept help from others during this time in your life. Yes, the Alive stage has a totally different set of needs than Survive, but you'll still need some help. Maybe you need help with the yard work or picking your kids up from school while you're at work. Maybe you need help making sense of the budget and managing your family's finances. Maybe you're suddenly a single father and have no idea how to help your teenage daughter with certain "embarrassing" issues. Whatever it is, do not be scared to ask for help. You aren't a failure for needing help every now and then, and the people who love you want to help. Let them.

Step **8**: Beware of Negative Coping Mechanisms

As we recover from a tragic loss and try to find some semblance of normalcy in our new lives, it can be tempting to medicate our grief with a number of unhealthy—and outright dangerous—coping mechanisms. I've talked to many people who turned to drugs and alcohol to dull the intense feelings of pain they were experiencing. Others mentioned going on wild shopping sprees to take their mind off their loss. Some did a complete home makeover, filling their homes with all-new furniture and décor they couldn't afford, saying they *needed* to spend money they didn't really have in order to feel comfortable in their homes. Still others coped by withdrawing from society and isolating themselves from loved ones so they wouldn't have to deal with "the look" or talk about their feelings. While I can understand the root cause of these varied reactions, we cannot allow ourselves to avoid dealing with the emotional aftermath of our loss. A well-timed distraction is often *exactly* what we need, but we cannot live a life full of distractions. Our pain *must* be faced head-on if we want to truly find happiness and joy again.

Show Yourself Grace

In conclusion, it is important to be gentle with yourself as you walk through the Alive season of your grief journey. While your life may start looking like normal, there is still a long way to go. You are still healing, so give yourself some grace. Be patient. The fact is, you *will* screw up and embarrass yourself a time or two. Or three. Or four thousand. You will think you're losing it at times. You'll start weeping while paying your electric bill or taking out the trash or brushing your child's hair because you'll remember that your loved one used to take care of that for you. All of that is okay. This is your time to transition. You're transitioning back into life and, in many cases, figuring out what your life will look like from now on. You won't get it right at first. It takes time, so give yourself plenty of it.

Jesus modeled grace in every sense of the word. From a Christian perspective, grace means unwarranted or unearned favor. That is, God shows His grace to us by loving and caring for us—going so far as to save us from our sins—even though we didn't (or couldn't) do anything to *deserve* it. I encourage you to treat yourself the same way. Love yourself. Care for yourself. Be patient with yourself. Say kind things to yourself. Do loving things for yourself. Even when you don't feel like you deserve it, even when you don't feel like you have anything to offer anyone, show grace to yourself. Try to see yourself the way God sees you: as a precious, perfect man or woman, created in His image, and worthy of love. Because that's exactly who and what you are.

So, where do we go from here? That's the best news I have to share: Life isn't just about surviving or relearning how to live; it's about *thriving* in every sense of the word. We'll discuss this magnificent season of the healing journey in the following two chapters as we finish the Survive-Alive-Thrive model with a breakdown of the third and final stage, Thrive.

Questions for Discussion

1. While still full of responsibilities, the Alive stage gives you more elbow room than the more tightly packed season of Survive. How would you compare your life in Alive to your experiences during Survive?

2. Most people report feeling overwhelmed during the Alive stage. What new collisions have you had in Alive as your new responsibilities, emotional responses, and outward reactions/manifestations swirl around your new life?

3. What has been your greatest emotional response during the Alive stage? How has that impacted your outward reactions/manifestations?

4. Have you experienced the conflict between *moving on* and *hanging on*? How so?

5. What positive emotional responses have you noticed following your loss? Examples might include closer relationships, a sense of gratitude for others, and so on.

6. What action step has been the most helpful for you as you've transitioned into the Alive stage?

7. What challenges have you faced in either starting counseling or considering counseling to work through your loss?

8. How has your loss experience impacted your physical body? Examples might include fatigue, illness, weight fluctuations, headaches, high blood pressure, and so forth. What steps have you taken to mitigate these issues?

9. In what ways have you or could you serve others as part of your own healing journey? What impact has that made or could that make?

10. Many people report changes in their routines and activities as they cope with loss. Have you been doing more (or less) of previous activities? Can you identify those changes that are positive and/or those that you should watch carefully?

Chapter 10

THE THRIVE STAGE

Part 1: A Full and Rewarding Life

*I*S IT EVEN POSSIBLE?

Can you experience a happy, giving, busy, joyful, fulfilling life after you've lost someone who truly meant the world to you? Can you love again after the death of a spouse? Can you find your footing after the death of a parent? Can you still be an active, ever-present parent to your other children after you've suffered the loss of one precious child? Can you truly and fully love your life after going through a heart-wrenching loss?

Can you *thrive*?

Yes. Yes, you can.

At the beginning of this journey, as we found ourselves in the Survive stage, we were just trying to get from one day to the next and deal with the trauma of our loss. Over time and with dedicated self-care, we entered the Alive stage where we started to balance the demands of life with the healing we needed to reclaim our lives. In the Alive sections, we discussed steps and tactics to help us approach our healing process in a healthy way that enables us to maintain a close connection to our loss experience without having our lives controlled by that loss. That doesn't mean we're in denial; we know we've been through a terrible loss. How could we not? However, we're learning to *live* with our loss. It is and always will be a part of us, so … now what?

Nobody I've ever spoken with wants to stop in the Alive stage, simply existing and functioning without experiencing the richness, beauty, and utter joy that life has to offer. We all want more in our lives regardless of what we've been through in the past. Of the three stages we've discussed in the Survive-Alive-Thrive model, Thrive is the only one that is truly optional. You can *want* it, as we all do, but to truly thrive, you have to embrace the opportunity to *choose* it and *work* towards it.

As you've been progressing on this healing journey, you just might look up one day and realize something has changed. Getting up in the morning may be easier. Sleeping through the night may be normal. These may seem like simple things, but they are huge milestones on the path to healing. These daily joys may give way to even bigger surprises—earmarks that you've stepped into the richness of the Thrive stage.

Where You Are and What You're Facing

In this chapter, we'll explore what it's like to begin experiencing hope and happiness on the journey after loss. I will identify the unique earmarks of the Thrive stage. It is my hope that these will help you understand and *celebrate* that you have progressed to this stage on your journey. If you are not yet at this stage, my hope is you will embrace the knowledge that you *can* and *will* experience the happiness and joy of this season in the future.

As with the previous stages, I will also review several of the most common challenges associated with this season and what you can expect to encounter as you continue the healing process. It's important to note that transitioning to a season where you are experiencing a full and rewarding life does not mean that you will not go through setbacks and deal with heartache and pain along the way. Life can be tough and it's not a matter of *if* you'll experience challenges and setbacks; it's a matter of *when*. In that context, this chapter identifies some of the key challenges of the Thrive stage as experienced in my personal journey and by others who have shared their stories.

Finding Yourself in the Thrive Stage

As it is when transitioning from each season of the Survive-Alive-Thrive journey, there is no timeline for arriving at the Thrive stage. There is only *your* time. As previously noted, the stages of Survive-Alive-Thrive are interconnected on the model graphic. The space shared by the stage's circles represent time spent coexisting in the adjacent stages. Like we said before, the transition within the grieving and healing process—now from Alive to Thrive—is not a clean- or clear-cut graduation of linear accomplishment; rather, it's a gradual transition as your grieving process progresses over time. In fact, it is fully expected we'll toggle emotionally from Thrive to Alive and back as we engage and are impacted by the challenges life presents. As such, it's helpful to remember that this is not a *destination*— it is a *journey*.

While I can't give a complete list of every earmark, I have listed several worth celebrating and embracing as you find yourself living a full and rewarding life in the Thrive stage of your healing journey.

THRIVE STAGE OVERVIEW

HALLMARKS OF THE SEASON	WHAT THAT CAN MEAN/LOOK LIKE
1 CATCHING YOURSELF LAUGHING	Moments of unexpected, pure laughter
	Laughing at funny memories that you shared with your lost loved one
	Abilty to feel your lost loved one laughing with you
2 REDISCOVERING A CAPACITY FOR LOVE	Ability to feel the richness of new love without guilt
	The result of focused attention, self-care, and healing
	New love a possibility, not a requirement for Thrive
3 PROLONGED PERIODS OF HAPPINESS	Comfortable in new routines
	Life seems to be flowing again
	Realization that you haven't felt deep sadness in a while
4 BECOMING SOCIALLY ACTIVE AGAIN	Fully engaged with your relationships
	See yourself as a valuable, contributing member of society
5 FRIENDS STOP BEING AWKWARD AROUND YOU	You haven't seen "the look" in a while
	Friends aren't walking on eggshells around you
	People feel comfortable talking about the person you lost

HALLMARKS OF THE SEASON	WHAT THAT CAN MEAN/LOOK LIKE
6 CRYING HAPPY TEARS	Your relationship with tears has matured
	Tears slip out briefly without the deep feeling of sadness
	Abilty to smile as you wipe a stray tear and think about the person you lost
7 WANTING TO HELP OTHERS	Develop a great capacity for helping others
	New empathy and compassion for people in pain
	Opportunities to serve people going through a similar experience
8 SEEING THE JOY IN LIFE	Ability to see the beauty in everyday life

Hallmark **1**: Catching Yourself Laughing

About a year and a half after Victoria's death, my son and I took a ski trip at a Colorado ski resort that we used to visit as a family while he was growing up. On the slopes one day, we came around a particular turn and Andersen stopped and said, "Hey, Dad! Isn't this the place?"

Andersen grew up skiing, so he's an expert. I'm pretty good. Victoria, who grew up in Florida, had a more difficult time learning the ropes. She worked her way up to intermediate level, but she still had quite a few accidents in the snow during those regular ski trips when my son was younger. One year, Andersen and I came down a slope and around a turn and stopped to wait on Victoria to catch up. We looked back and saw her flying towards the turn. It was clear she wasn't going to make it. In a panic, she headed toward the rope barrier she thought could slow her down. It didn't. Instead, she sailed under the rope and disappeared behind an embankment. Andersen and I hurried over and looked down the ledge to find her lying face-first in a three-foot mound of fresh powder. When we called out to her, she rolled over, looked up at us, and said, "I'm okay! It's soft!"

My son and I looked at each other and burst out laughing. We couldn't help it. It looked like Frosty the Snowman had a ski accident! Victoria, always a great sport, started laughing as well as she climbed back up to join us. It was a precious memory for our family for years to come, something we often spontaneously started laughing about around the dinner table and with friends.

Neither Andersen or I had mentioned that ski story since his mother died, but that day on the slopes, we found ourselves right back on that same sharp curve. The rope was still there. The embankment still led to a mound of fresh, soft snow—no doubt ready to catch the next wayward novice. When my son pointed it out to me that day, we looked at each other and burst out laughing, just as hard and joyfully as we did the day Victoria crashed on the mountain. We could picture every detail of the accident in our minds and were overcome with the joy of how funny that image was and what a cherished memory it had been to us all those years. With tears of laughter in our eyes, we each came to our senses about the same time and just looked at each other, realizing what had just happened. We were experiencing joy by reliving a memory of Victoria. We were full-on laughing at something she did … and she would have *loved* that. He and I both felt her there, laughing right along with us that day.

That unexpected laughter is, I think, one of the most critical indicators that you've stepped into the Thrive stage. There was a point not too long ago when I never thought I'd laugh again. I especially never thought I'd be able to laugh at something my wife once did—at least not without following a momentary giggle with tears of sadness. But then, unexpectedly, we catch ourselves in these surprise moments of levity, when we can feel the person we've lost laughing right alongside us. It may feel strange at first—that airy feeling of joy without a corresponding heaviness of loss. That day on the slopes was the first time my son and I realized we could remember the joy and humor of his mother's life without reliving the trauma we'd experienced by her death. In retrospect, that experience was a big flashing sign that said, "Welcome to Thrive, Mark! We're glad you're here!"

Hallmark 2: Rediscovering a Capacity for Love

While every loss is painful, there is something uniquely devastating about the death of a spouse. It strikes at our most precious, intimate relationship and can leave us feeling like a huge part of us died along with our spouse. Several months after Victoria died, I felt a swell of conflicting emotions. On one hand, I ached for female companionship. Victoria and I had been together for three decades, and I loved being part of a committed relationship. I have always believed I was made to be a husband and partner, so when my wife was taken from me, I felt like the husband piece of me died as well. I couldn't imagine living the rest of my life without sharing that connection with a woman.

On the other hand, I was completely heartbroken. It felt as though every drop of love I'd ever felt for her suddenly turned into pure pain. In a way, it seemed like my heart—perhaps even love itself—had betrayed me. As I made my way through Survive, I couldn't imagine ever loving again. Though I desperately wanted it, it was easy to believe that I'd never again feel love's exhilarating touch.

And then....

I took the step and began to date. Although I was blessed to meet several special and supportive women in Connecticut, those relationships were not meant to be, and I moved to the Nashville area to be closer to family and effectively start over and focus on this book. Victoria had been gone over two years, and I was in a new town where I knew virtually no one. I thought online dating would be a way for me to make new friends while getting to know my new town. Two birds with one stone, right? Though I wasn't opposed to finding new love, I don't know that I was *looking* for it. But five months later love found me, nonetheless. Melyn and I "matched" online and began talking by email and phone. When we met in person for dinner, I immediately felt something stir in my heart—something I hadn't felt in a long time. Yes, she was beautiful, and also bright, accomplished, funny, and intensely interesting. Our first date flew by as we talked for hours. So did the second date. And the third. Before I knew what was happening, I fell in love with her. And as I did more than three decades earlier with Victoria, I fell *hard,* and I fell *fast.* I suppose that's how I'm wired. When God drops an amazing and wonderful woman in front of me, I act!

As I write this, Melyn and I have been married for a year or so after dating for a year and a half. The COVID-19 pandemic threw our wedding plans out the window, but we pressed on by having a small ceremony with a few close friends and family members at our new home. We even had monogrammed face masks to commemorate the occasion—in such a crazy time, you might as well have fun with it.

Melyn is truly one of the great miracles of my life. In her, I discovered that "Mark the partner and husband" wasn't dead or permanently damaged after all. I was joyfully reminded that my capacity for love didn't end with Victoria's life. Furthermore, I am able to experience the richness of life and love with Melyn without feeling like I'm dishonoring Victoria. This didn't happen by accident, of course. I firmly believe that this capacity to love was returned to me as a result of the intentional healing journey I undertook for years before meeting Melyn. I pursued counseling, prayed endlessly for God's help and direction, walked with other hurting people, explored my soul, faced my pain, got my house in order, and every other step we've discussed. And somewhere along that road, God brought me Melyn. It was a wonderful, beautiful surprise.

Now, if you've lost a spouse, I want to be clear that your journey may not take you in the same direction. Whether you were married six months or sixty years, you may be perfectly content to live the rest of your life as a widow or widower. And truly, that can be just as beautiful if that's what you choose. The power here, the thing that I'd call an earmark of the Thrive stage, isn't necessarily engaging in a new love relationship. Rather, it's recognizing your *capacity* for love. It's understanding and accepting the fact that your heart lives on, that you have the freedom and capacity to give and receive love again—if you want to.

Hallmark 3: Enjoying Prolonged Periods of Happiness

One of the most exciting hallmarks of the Thrive stage is what I call "prolonged periods of happiness." This usually starts happening before we even realize it. We are deep into the Alive stage, and life is flowing. We're back in a groove, we feel comfortable in our new routines and way of life, we've made new relationships, we've entered into a new phase with our existing relationships, and things are generally rocking along. And then, out of the blue, you realize, *Hey, I haven't felt that deep sadness in months.* That realization may admittedly be a bit unsettling for some, but it's a clear sign that your heart and mind have moved into Thrive territory.

Hallmark 4: Becoming Socially Active Again

During the Alive stage, you began hanging out with friends again and dipped your toes in the social waters, trying to get a feel for what your new life might look like, but now in Thrive, you're all-in with your relationships. You see and talk to friends regularly, you stay in touch with your extended family, you may be involved in a church community, and you have people in your life who want to see you (and whom you want to see). This doesn't mean you've suddenly become an extrovert if you weren't before; it just means you are no longer hiding in your home or actively avoiding the rest of the world. You embrace the fact that you are a valuable person and an important part of your community. You know you have something to offer society, and you are ready to share it with your small part of the world.

Hallmark **5**: Friends Stop Being Awkward Around You

When our lives fall apart at the start of Survive, it's as though the shrapnel has hit the ground and covered a thirty-foot radius around us. For a while, whenever someone breaches that zone, you can tell they are carefully watching their step. They're guarding every word. They're holding back some thoughts while sharing others that are unhelpful at best and downright foolish at worst. They're tiptoeing around the obvious: that our lives have changed forever. Though well-meaning, most people simply don't know how to talk to hurting friends. So they do this weird dance that makes everyone uncomfortable for a while.

But then, at some point, the weirdness fades. You stop getting "the look" and start getting big, bright smiles. Your best friend stops giving you tender, slow, mournful side hugs and goes back to the full, manly, goofy bear hugs you've exchanged for years. And, of course, my personal favorite: people stop trying to buy you dinner and you go back to simply hanging out and taking care of your own bill like you used to. I've never been so content to pay for a steak dinner in my life as I was after my buddies stopped babying me!

Similarly, people regain their freedom to talk about the person you lost. Our friends and family have so many hilarious stories about Victoria, but they were all too skittish to even mention her name for a long time. As time passed and I regained my sense of self, though, I noticed the people around me brought her up more often. At some point, we started reminding each other of funny things she did and telling the wonderful stories of her life. Even though this was a priority for me as early as her memorial service ten days after her death, it took a long time for people to get comfortable saying her name around me. It may have been for the best for a while, but at some point, I missed hearing how much she meant to people. Her life was an adventure, and her stories need to be told!

Hallmark **6**: Crying Happy Tears

In Survive, we can cry buckets of tears, almost like we're expelling the sorrow in our hearts through our eyes. In Alive, we still cry sad tears, though not quite as often. This especially happens when we bump into a cherished memory, hit our first key holidays post-loss, or face a responsibility that our loved one once handled for us. As we enter Thrive, though, our relationship with tears has matured. We still feel free to cry sad tears, but those episodes are fewer and further between. More importantly, we discover the beauty of happy tears. This most often happens to me when I'm telling someone about Victoria or remembering an experience that we shared that genuinely makes my heart happy. Tears still slip out— maybe because I'm a pretty emotional guy—but they feel different now. I've learned how to smile, laugh, and cry all at the same time, and it feels perfectly natural. And unlike the tears I cried in the earlier stages, these moments do not derail my entire day or render me socially worthless. I can wipe a tear, say hello to Victoria in my heart, smile, and move on with my day. When you can greet your lost loved one with a smile and a few happy tears as a normal, healthy part of your day, you've probably crossed the threshold into Thrive.

Hallmark **7**: Wanting to Help Others

Early in your healing journey, it was probably difficult for you to show up for anyone else. Rather, you depended on the kindness of others just as much as I depended on the steady stream of lasagna dinners from my church family. As you move through the Survive-Alive-Thrive stages, though, you develop a great capacity for serving others. More importantly, you develop a *desire* to serve and an *empathy* for the pain others are going through. I have heard from many people how they began serving in some capacity related to their area of loss. People who have lost loved ones to cancer volunteer in cancer wards. Families of suicide victims lead support groups for others going through that particular heartache. Parents who have lost children mentor other families new to the struggle. Many have reported that serving in these ways became the most personally fulfilling thing they've ever done. There are so many wonderful ways to serve your community, and your experience—as painful as it was—has uniquely equipped you to bless another person in need. That is a tremendous honor and responsibility, and it is one we begin to embrace as we venture into Thrive.

Hallmark **8**: Seeing the Joy in Life

Finally, Thrive is marked by an ability once again to see the joy in life. This may sound trite, but those of us who have been through the dark valley of loss understand how difficult it can be to rediscover the joys in every moment of life.

As I sit here in my home office writing this, my thoughts are on my mother-in-law, who died in the next room after being moved into our home for the final stage of her hospice care. During those hard, final days, my wife and I were amazed at her attitude. Her mind had been severely impacted by a tragic accident and subsequent head trauma, so there were many days when she would say things that were not logical or rational. Then there were moments of clarity when her razor-sharp wit came blazing back in full force. Through it all, Melyn soaked up every moment she had left with her beloved mother. Sure, we've faced no small amount of sadness over her death, but our home was filled with as many smiles and blessings as tears during her final days.

All of life—up to and including death—is a thing of beauty and wonder. One of the greatest gifts of Thrive is the ability to see it *all*.

Facing the Challenges of Thrive

Just because you're thriving at this stage doesn't mean every day is perfect. Far from it, in fact. Every season of Survive-Alive-Thrive includes ups and downs, wins and losses, good days and bad days—even Thrive. However, I pray at this stage that your challenges start to feel far more manageable than they did in Survive or even Alive. At this point, the difficulties in your life should start to feel more like *normal* life, rather than distinctly tied to your loss. However, there will be days and situations that bring your loss right back to the forefront of your mind. Let's review some of the most common challenges we'll face at this stage.

NOTABLE CHALLENGES OF THE THRIVE STAGE	
NOTABLE CHALLENGES	**WHAT THAT CAN MEAN/LOOK LIKE**
1 BENCHMARK DAYS AND SPECIAL OCCASIONS	Annual reminders of the person you lost Question of how to mark special days moving forward
2 UNEXPECTED EMOTIONAL TRIGGERS	Caught off guard by random reminders in unlikely times and places Suddenly crying somewhere where you shared a special memory Uncertainty of what reminders and surprises each day holds

NOTABLE CHALLENGES	WHAT THAT CAN MEAN/LOOK LIKE
3 NEW RELATIONSHIPS	Accepting a new person in a role someone you love once filled
	Getting used to a new stepparent or romantic partner
	Resisting the inclination to compare a new spouse to a deceased spouse
4 NEW SETBACKS AND LOSSES	The wolf is still at the door
	Possibility of going through a similar loss all over again

Challenge **1**: Benchmark Days and Special Occasions

Every life is made up of a handful of "benchmark days," or occasions that are uniquely special for a person or family. These are things such as birthdays and wedding anniversaries, not to mention common holidays such as Thanksgiving and Christmas that, no doubt, remind us of special times and family traditions we shared with our loved one. I'm afraid these dates don't drop off the calendar just because the person we love is gone. And of course, there are the less celebratory benchmark days, such as the anniversary of someone's death or the anniversary of an agonizing medical diagnosis. These dates can become extremely painful every year if we're not intentional about how we approach them.

For example, May 25 is a benchmark day for me. That's the anniversary of Victoria's death. That date would be hard enough under any circumstance, but the details of my experience on that date in 2016 make it especially difficult. Every year on that day, part of me remembers the events related to her death. It's visceral. I can still remember the pain of that experience, even now that I'm well into Thrive.

I feel other things on other special occasions. Every November 23 will remind me of eloping with Victoria in 1995 when we got married on the beach in Mexico. Every Mother's Day will remind me of the excitement we shared when we were expecting our son and the incredible way she loved Andersen. Every October 28—Andersen's birthday—will remind me of watching in awe as Victoria delivered our child into the world. Every Thanksgiving will remind me of standing with Victoria to declare my commitment to Christ at our family dinner in 1999. Between dating and marriage, we were together for thirty years. That's a lot of memories scattered all throughout the calendar, and the meaning attached to those dates didn't die with her. No matter how much I've healed, no matter how much I love and adore Melyn, those dates will always remind me of Victoria. I'm so blessed to now be married to a woman who not only understands that but who actively encourages me to honor those memories and the connection I have to those dates.

Whether your loss is fresh or years old, I know you understand how powerful these annual reminders are. With time and healing, they can and will become beautiful milestones, but that certainly doesn't happen quickly or easily.

Challenge **2**: Unexpected Emotional Triggers

While we usually see benchmark dates coming, there are other emotional triggers that will seemingly hit us from out of the blue. These are innocent reminders of our loved one or difficult circumstances that will simply pop up randomly as we go about our lives. For example, Andersen and I finding ourselves in the exact spot where Victoria fell into a snow drift was an emotional trigger. Fortunately, we were in a healthy emotional place and welcomed the memory. Other times, we're hit with reminders that cut a bit more deeply. For example, one widow I interviewed described how she was progressing nicely through her healing journey when she suddenly found herself in tears standing in a car dealer's showroom. The concerned service manager asked her what was wrong, and she explained that her husband always took the lead on servicing the family cars, and this was the first time she'd had to bring in her car since his death. Standing there in the queue, surrounded by busy salespeople and other car owners, she was suddenly overcome with a rush of emotion. She was feeling his loss in a new way— one she never saw coming.

The same thing can happen when we visit a vacation spot we once shared with our loved one, when someone brings up a funny story about him or her that we didn't know or hadn't thought of in a while, when we're unpacking a box and find an old photo album, and when we're simply going about our daily lives. Every day holds the potential to surprise us with an emotional run-in with our loved one, and these encounters can be loving, happy, funny, sad, or heartbreaking. We simply do not know what surprises each day holds. What we *do* know, however, is that these surprises pack an emotional punch we may not be ready for, no matter how far into Thrive we are.

Challenge ❸: New Relationships

Another challenge is getting used to new relationships after you've lost someone. For example, your mother may remarry after your father's death, and your new stepfather might be a bit of a loudmouth whereas your dad was quiet and unassuming. Or perhaps you remarry after the death of your spouse, and your new husband or wife has totally different interests than your loved one did. This situation can be unsettling to say the least, and it surprises many people (although it really shouldn't). Every individual is unique, and we each bring these unique characteristics into our relationships. After a while, we get used to loving someone a certain way, in a way that honors and recognizes his or her unique interests and personality. But then, we're suddenly thrown into a new relationship, and we discover that the way we're used to loving our partner doesn't work anymore. Even if we've had thirty years of marriage experience, we feel like a relationship rookie because our new spouse doesn't respond to us the way our former spouse did. It can be quite a shock and terribly difficult, but we have to relearn how to engage with a new spouse or parent based on *that person's* particularities. This can be fertile ground for some groundshaking early disagreements in a new relationship.

Challenge ④: New Setbacks and Losses

I mentioned this in the previous chapters on Alive, but it's worth restating here from a Thrive perspective. Even when you are years into Thrive, the wolf is *still* at the door. You will continue to encounter new setbacks and losses—even new tragedies—as you progress throughout your healing journey. If you've tragically lost a child, for example, it's still possible to go through that nightmare all over again with another child. If you've lost a spouse, you could remarry and someday become *twice* widowed. If you've lost one friend to a terminal illness, you might still lose another in a car accident in the future. If you've beaten one form of cancer, you might still face another life-threatening disease years later. The bottom line is that the hits keep on coming, no matter who you are or where you are in the Survive-Alive-Thrive journey. In fact, it's not uncommon to be in the Thrive stage after one loss only to be thrown back into Survive after another. It's not a pleasant thought, but I'm afraid it's a basic fact of life.

Reengaging Life

In general, Thrive is marked by our reengaging life socially, emotionally, professionally, and relationally. It is a magnificent time where we truly feel like we've gotten a new lease on life filled with new opportunities, new relationships, new loves, new adventures, and a new purpose. None of these things disrespects the people we've lost. They'd *want* us to keep on living, to reengage life in a fresh, new, exciting way.

So how do we do that? We'll answer that in the following chapter, as we unpack Thrive's common emotional responses and some suggested action steps for making the most of this wonderful progression through the Survive-Alive-Thrive model.

Questions for Discussion

1. Do you believe it is even possible to thrive following a significant loss? What would that look like for you?

2. When I say that Thrive is the only stage you have to *choose* for yourself, do you agree with that statement? Why wouldn't *everyone* choose to thrive?

3. What earmarks made it clear that you had entered the Thrive stage? If you aren't there yet, what earmarks do you most look forward to as you enter this new stage?

4. In this chapter, Mark describes a time when he and his son enjoyed a good laugh together while remembering something his wife had done years earlier. Being able to laugh at that memory was a turning point for them. Have you had a similar experience in which you've been able to enjoy happy memories without feeling the pain of your loss all over again?

5. What does/would the "capacity to love again" mean for you in light of your loss?

6. Have your friends stopped being weird around you yet? How have your relationships changed or grown in the time since your loss?

7. What's been your biggest challenge as you enter into the Thrive stage?

8. List and describe your benchmark days and explain how you plan to recognize them moving forward.

9. What unexpected emotional triggers have surprised you as you've moved into Thrive?

10. What's the most intimidating thing you have faced or expect to face as you reengage life socially, emotionally, professionally, and relationally?

Chapter 11

THE THRIVE STAGE

Part 2: Full Steam Ahead

*I*N THE PREVIOUS CHAPTER, WE BEGAN OUR EXPLORATION INTO THE marvelous world of Thrive. We began to understand what it means to thrive by identifying the earmarks of the Thrive stage and exploring the challenges we'll face even this far into our healing journey. Now let's continue our journey into this third and final stage of the Survive-Alive-Thrive model by looking at our most common emotional responses during this season, suggested action steps for making the most of it, and ways we can better understand and serve others going through this part of their journey.

What to Expect in This Chapter

In this chapter, we'll explore how our emotional reactions have continued to evolve now that we've transitioned to the Thrive stage of our journey from loss to hope and happiness. Although there are many reasons to celebrate when arriving at this season, there will still be challenges in life because our loss has become a part of us, and we will always carry it with us moving forward.

The emotional responses listed in this section again fall into two categories: challenging and healthy responses. As we are now thriving in a full and rewarding life, this section's list starts with *healthy* emotional responses we are likely experiencing. As it is with each chapter committed to the Survive-Alive-Thrive journey, the goal remains to simply identify with your own personal experience and to embrace the idea that you are not alone in what you're going through. While we do not necessarily experience *all* the responses listed, nor do we need to, there are likely those provided to which you can relate.

Finally, like with the other stages, you'll find recommended strategies and healthy steps to help keep you engaged in a healthy, full, and rewarding life. I hope and pray that these will help you as you continue to thrive at this stage of your healing journey.

Emotional Responses to Loss: Thrive Stage

In the previous chapters on Survive and Alive, we began our examination of emotional responses and outward reactions/manifestations by looking at our *challenging* responses. That made sense in the first two stages, because those seasons are largely about mitigating the pain associated with close proximity to our loss, getting back on your feet, and fighting to reclaim your life. In Thrive, however, those difficult emotional moments become fewer and farther between. It only makes sense, then, that we'd start here by identifying the healthy, *positive* emotional responses we're likely to experience during the Thrive season. We will then explore ongoing potential *challenging* emotional responses that we can still find lurking even while thriving.

Again, this is not a test or contest to have more responses from one group or the other. The goal is simply to identify with your own personal experience and to embrace the idea that you are not alone in what you're going through.

THRIVE STAGE: EMOTIONAL RESPONSES SNAPSHOT	
POSITIVE RESPONSES	**WHAT THAT CAN MEAN/LOOK LIKE**
1 RE-EVALUATING YOUR PURPOSE	Begin to ask, "Is this all there is?"
	Risk trading *purpose* for *comfort*
	Dream of what you can do with your life and dare to actually do it
2 BECOMING RESILIENT	Develop a thick skin around pain and loss
	Able to endure more than you ever imagined

Positive Emotional Responses

As we saw in the previous chapter, thriving doesn't mean you have a totally problem-free life or that you're spending every day dancing on the silver lining of cloud nine. However, thriving *is* about living and living *well*. It's about reengaging in your life, jumping in with both feet, and giving yourself the freedom and space to enjoy who you are, where you are, what you're doing, and who you're with. Your experience of the Thrive stage will include a tremendous amount of personal growth, specifically in two areas: purpose and resilience.

Positive Response ❶: Reevaluating Your Purpose

As many of us enter Thrive and get to a point of happiness years after our loss, we may begin to wonder if we're "done" with the healing process. We may think, *Well, I'm at peace with my loss and I seem to be doing pretty well. Is this all there is?* That question—*is this all there is?*—can begin chipping away at us, leading us into either a bout of frustration and dissatisfaction or into a whole new adventure of self-discovery.

Rick Warren's bestselling book *The Purpose Driven Life* challenges us to thrive and find joy by defining the purpose for which God has put us on this earth. And in my experience, few things initiate a search for our unique purpose more than going through a tragic loss. We tend to get so settled in our lives that we unknowingly trade *purpose* for *comfort*. It's easy to fall into our routines and the safety of our relationships and assume we're living our best lives. But then when tragedy strikes and our world is turned upside down, we're forced to reexamine who we are, what we're doing, what we're contributing to society, and what we truly want out of life. This typically strikes during the Thrive stage. During Survive and Alive, the goal is to simply get back on our feet. During Thrive, though, we may not be satisfied simply to stand still. We may even feel the urge to *run*. In these times, we begin to question our true purpose in life.

This is both a blessing and a challenge of the Thrive season. When done with a level head and proper preparation, this quest for purpose can lead to exciting, fulfilling new adventures. When done spontaneously as an emotional reaction, it can lead to mistakes we'll regret and that can hurt the ones we love.

For example, I was approached about writing this book just six months after Victoria's death, but I was well-advised by a trusted mentor to put the book on the backburner for a while and focus on my healing. Two years later, confident that I was comfortably in the Thrive season, I began to take seriously my new dream of walking alongside people during their time of grief and loss. After much research and planning, I launched a nonprofit organization centered around connecting grieving individuals. I spent a year working with professionals to develop the Survive-Alive-Thrive website, audio interviews, podcasts, and community. I sought a publisher and editor to help me finally put this book together. And today, I truly feel like I'm living my purpose—my *new* purpose—of walking with and loving people through their darkest days.

Now, at every point in this journey of self-discovery, I wanted to move faster. I felt compelled to do more, jump into action, make drastic changes, spend more money, and write a book quickly. And if I had done these things, I would have completely sabotaged my family, my finances, my relationships, my future, my healing, and the new purpose God was unfolding before me. I am so grateful for what He has called me to do with the rest of my life, but I could have wrecked it all by moving too quickly. Fortunately, He not only gave me a vision for my new purpose but also trusted advisors who continually encouraged me to slow down and respect my healing process—even after I had entered Thrive. I would now like to do the same for you.

Along with this new sense of purpose comes new energy and optimism. You not only begin to dream of *what* you can do with your life, but you feel the inner strength to actually do it and you can picture yourself being successful. Purpose, energy, and optimism are all lacking during the early days, weeks, and months after a loss. In fact, it may be years before you're settled enough into your new life that you're even capable of dreaming again. But then, slowly but surely, the fog lifts on the horizon. You can see further and clearer than you have in a while, and a new purpose starts to take shape. That's the far reaches of Thrive calling you to think bigger, dream better, and walk bolder. Listen to it.

Positive Response **2**: Becoming Resilient

The term *thick skin* is thrown around a lot, but have you ever stopped to think what that expression literally means? Imagine you were suddenly moved out of your comfy desk job and out into the sun-drenched, sweat-soaked world of landscaping. You trade your keyboard and mouse for a weed eater and rake. Rather than lounging in an ergonomic office chair or improving your posture at a standing desk, you're crawling through mulch on your hands and knees. You spend eight or nine hours a day working with your hands, carrying heavy equipment, pushing mowers, trimming hedges, and sawing tree limbs. Tell me: how do you think your hands would feel after the first week? My guess is they'd be a sore, cramped, and bloody mess. Those of us who work indoors take our soft hands for granted. They get the job done for computer work. Maybe a few years of playing guitar or another instrument has given us a callous or two. But, by and large, we've got soft, delicate hands with thin skin.

After a week of working outdoors, our hands have taken a beating. By week two, we might have gotten used to the routines, but we're still struggling with splinters and blisters. A few months in, however, we probably wouldn't notice any discomfort at all. Our hands would have adapted to the new conditions, developing calluses to protect us from our harsh new reality. Those calluses are literally patches of thick skin. Our bodies are designed to build up a suit of armor to defend us from new threats and painful new conditions. I believe our hearts and minds are designed to do the exact same thing.

Working our way through a loss—and I mean *literally* working our way with intentionality through the healing process—causes us to develop resilience. We are able to endure more than we ever thought possible because we've already endured the worst life has to offer. You can handle tougher and tougher things with greater grace because you've already survived the unthinkable. For example, when I first began dating after Victoria's death, a friend came to me with sincere concern in his voice. He asked, "Mark, are you sure you want to date again? What if it doesn't go well? What if you lose this person? Won't that break your heart? Won't that break *you*?"

I literally laughed out loud. I replied, "Listen, I now know there is *nothing* I could ever go through that I can't handle. Once you've gone through the fires of hell, you learn not to fear it. You respect it. You appreciate it. But you never fear it again."

Now, have I been hurt in relationships since Victoria's death? Absolutely. Did those painful situations break me? Absolutely not. I'm not claiming to be invulnerable by any stretch of the imagination, but I know without a doubt that I have already faced the most horrifying moment of my life. I know I will have more challenges and losses in my life, but my healing journey has taught me that I can handle them. And so can you.

Challenging Emotional Responses

Just as there are new challenges throughout this season, there will be new potentially challenging emotional responses as well. However, at this stage, these responses are less likely to wreck your life than they are in the earlier stages. Instead, the bigger threat of unhealthy emotional responses during Thrive is their capacity to undermine your ability to thrive in your new life.

THRIVE STAGE EMOTIONAL RESPONSES SNAPSHOT	
CHALLENGING RESPONSES	WHAT THAT CAN MEAN/LOOK LIKE
1 INSECURITY ABOUT YOUR NEW LIFE	Worry that your new life is "less-than" or a backup plan
	Danger of comparing your life to the lives of others
	Risk falling into the trap of comparing your new life to your old life

CHALLENGING RESPONSES	WHAT THAT CAN MEAN/LOOK LIKE
2 LONELINESS	Times of feeling lonely specifically for the person you lost
	Danger of rushing into a new relationship to avoid feeling alone
3 TOO MUCH OF A GOOD THING	Overindulging in food, alcohol, shopping, and other avoidance activities
	Risk of overmedicating rather than fully addressing your pain
	Potential to undermine your healing in the name of "treating" yourself
4 COMPLACENCY	Never a time when you've "made it"
	Healing is a progressive journey that will never stop
	Risk of getting sloppy with the healing process

Challenging Response **1**: Insecurity About Your New Life

Moving from the old way of life to a new way is shocking for most of us. That's why I suggest people in Survive and even early in Alive don't even try to imagine the long-term implications of their loss quite yet. Trying to figure out the long-term plan too soon can derail the short-term survival mode we all need to go through in the weeks and months after a big loss. However, as we settle into Thrive and are therefore enjoying a full and rewarding life, we must be on guard against a creeping sense of insecurity that can undermine our enjoyment.

By *insecurity*, I mean two different applications. The first is a sense that our new life is *"less-than"* compared to the life we once lived. We can get stuck in a "Plan B" way of thinking that always compares where we are *now* to where we were *then* or where we *thought* we'd be now. Or even if we're happy and fulfilled with our new lives, we can get distracted by what our peers have and start to play the comparison game—something that is all too common and far too easy in today's world of social media. If you've had to downgrade your home and lifestyle as a result of your loss, for example, you may feel insecure about having less than your friends or even less than you once had yourself. This is even more tragic if you lose a spouse and remarry, and then you start to compare your new husband or wife to the one you lost. That's a dangerous game and unfair to everyone involved.

Your previous life deserves to be remembered and cherished, but it cannot become a specter haunting the life you're now living and building. We must be mindful, then, to take the best of those good times with us into our new lives, not as a point of comparison, but as happy memories and healthy goals for the life before us.

The second application of an insecurity response is that things have turned out so much *better* than you could have imagined following your loss that you are terrified you can lose it all over again. Tragically, the fear driving such insecurity is not unique to those who have found happiness following loss. Many people experience guilt in these circumstances, wondering if they deserve such blessings. Others can become prisoners of their own success and are so consumed with holding onto their perceived happiness of success that they fail to live a rich and rewarding life. The key to overcoming these challenges is trusting that God will always be with you no matter the outcome. It is my hope that the resilience you have achieved through your loss journey far exceeds any sense of insecurity related to experiencing another loss. Of course, your faith/worldview is integral to mitigating this response, and we will explore God's role in that context in section 3, "Greater Than That."

Challenging Response ❷: Loneliness

Feeling lonely is a natural part of experiencing loss, especially if you've lost a spouse or romantic partner. I've addressed this issue several times in this book, and it's pretty clear that I'm a relationship-centered guy who thrives on connections with other people. For me, the need to establish that kind of heart connection with another woman was deeply important once I fully healed from Victoria's death. God blessed me beyond imagination with Melyn—and I tell her so every day. However, remarriage may not be in the cards for you. Many widows and widowers have zero interest in ever engaging in a romantic relationship with another person, and there is absolutely nothing wrong with that. New romance is not a prerequisite for thriving. It's something that *may* happen. Or it may not. It's something you *may* want. Or you may not. It's something that *may* surprise you, even if you weren't looking for it. Or it may not.

Regardless of your intention to carry the old flame or light a new one, you will certainly face loneliness at times—even in Thrive. Further, even if you become happily remarried and are deeply in love with your new spouse, there will probably be times when you're especially lonely for the person you lost. That doesn't mean you're being emotionally unfaithful to your new love. It is just your heart's recognition that you deeply loved your lost spouse and you are grateful for the time you shared, whether it was two years or fifty-two years. You can't entwine your life with someone else's without that thread staying with you in some way for the rest of your life. It's nothing to be ashamed of or embarrassed about, and it's nothing for your new love interest to be jealous of. My advice here is to be honest with yourself and your new partner about what you're experiencing. If he or she becomes jealous or if you realize you're projecting your love for your lost spouse onto your new one, I suggest you seek counseling together. Do not let the ghost of your old marriage ruin your new one.

All that said, I should offer another caution here: Loneliness for your lost loved one is not a reason to rush into a new relationship with someone else. Marriage is sacred and is not to be taken lightly. Rebound relationships are filled with problems you won't be ready for early in your healing journey. Real, loving, committed relationships later in the process can be tricky enough to manage; you definitely don't want to add more emotional drama to your life when you're still struggling with your loss.

Challenging Response ❸: Too Much of a Good Thing

You should know what I mean when I caution you against "too much of a good thing." Rich foods, sweets, relaxation, alcohol, shopping, medication, and other luxuries can be wonderful things—in moderation. However, each of these things and more can easily become out-of-control coping mechanisms if we aren't careful. Our impatient, pleasure-minded brains can turn just about *anything* into an avoidance tool, something we use to placate or distract ourselves from the *real* issues that need attention. And when left unchecked for too long, each of these *good* things can become *terrible* things for our emotional and physical health.

I'll admit that a glass of red wine and a slice of chocolate cake can help take the edge off a bad day during our healing process. In fact, they are favorites of mine! If we left it there, there wouldn't be a problem. However, how often does this turn into a *nightly* glass of wine and slice of cake? And how often does *that* turn into a nightly *bottle* of wine and an *entire* cake? At that point, we've just introduced an alcohol and sugar problem (not to mention new health problems) into an already troubled situation.

We've previously identified the dangers of medicating your pain and engaging in unhealthy coping mechanisms as an avoidance strategy. While this is critical in the early days of your healing journey, you can't lose sight of it once you cross into Thrive. The potential to undermine your health and healing in the name of "treating yourself" is still there and still just as powerful.

Challenging Response ❹: Complacency

When I first introduced the Survive-Alive-Thrive model in chapter 5, I explained that it was progressive in nature. What I didn't make clear at that time is that you'll *never* stop progressing. You'll keep growing every day for the rest of your life. There will never be a time when you've "made it" in your healing journey, and there's no finish line you're racing toward. Instead, your progress is marked by daily victories and personal growth as you grow more fully throughout the Thrive stage.

Too often, people begin thriving and take their foot off the gas. They think they've *arrived* and therefore stop attending to their hearts and souls. They can get sloppy, frankly, and that's when new problems arise. In Thrive, it becomes more important than ever to guard against complacency because, again, the wolf is always at the door. Other bad things may (or, rather, *will*) happen. You need to be strong. You need to be ready. You need to continue your pursuit of healing and wholeness, being mindful of all the things we've discussed so far.

Suggested Steps for Continued Happiness

Congratulations are in order. You have reached the Thrive stage and are experiencing a full and rewarding life. Your loss experience is now a part of you in a healthy and balanced context! At this point in the journey, it is important that you guard against complacency and other undermining threats and dangers of the Thrive stage. How do we do that? To get you started, I've provided a list of suggested healthy steps to help you progress through your healing journey.

HEALTHY STEPS: NAVIGATING THE *THRIVE* STAGE	
HEALTHY STEPS	**WHAT THAT CAN MEAN/LOOK LIKE**
1 EMBRACE IMPORTANT BENCHMARK DATES	Celebrate rather than dread important dates and anniversaries Use these dates as oppportunities to celebrate the person you lost

HEALTHY STEPS	WHAT THAT CAN MEAN/LOOK LIKE
2 FULLY ENGAGE COMPANIONSHIP	Not necessarily about romantic relationships (though that is possible)
	Be an active part of society through groups, clubs, church, etc.
	Allow your healing journey to lead you back out into the world
3 TAKE CARE OF YOUR BODY	Plenty of rest, exercise, and good nutrition
	Prepare yourself physically and mentally for future losses
4 SHARE YOUR STORY, WISDOM, AND EXPERIENCE	Gives others the benefit of your experience
	Takes your own healing to the next level
	Many opportunities in person and online
5 PURSUE JOY	Recognition that joy is not only possible but likely
	Best expression of joy found in seeing your struggle through God's eyes

Step 1: Embrace Important Benchmark Dates

From a mental and emotional health standpoint, the first step I recommend is to embrace the important benchmark dates we mentioned in the previous chapter. Too often, these become days we dread. We can easily fall into an Ebenezer Scrooge mindset, grumbling, "Bah, humbug," whenever these special occasions arise. We may even avoid facing them altogether by staying off social media, not responding to calls or texts, and hiding inside on those days. I understand that reaction—especially early in the loss journey—but that doesn't sound like thriving behavior to me. Yes, these days hold the potential for pain, but they also contain the potential for celebration.

As you settle into thriving, be sure to leave room for honoring the person you lost in healthy, uplifting ways. For example, every year on Victoria's birthday, I post one of my favorite pictures of her on Facebook and celebrate her life and the impact she had on everyone she encountered. I also invite others to celebrate Victoria by commenting on the post so that we can all remember and honor her together. She was an incredible woman, wife, mother, daughter, sister, and friend who is dearly missed by so many. I wouldn't think to let her birthday go by without honoring her in some way and giving others the chance to join in.

That does not mean you should (or shouldn't) hold a vigil to commemorate the death of the person you lost. I know many people who host golf tournaments or other fundraising events to support related causes on benchmark dates as a way of honoring lost parents, spouses, siblings, or children. I salute those who embrace and focus on a powerful and positive message. In fact, I have found that a key to celebrating those we've lost is to focus on how they lived and the good they represented rather than on their death or loss.

It's also okay if you prefer to not dwell on a painful date associated with your loss. In my case, for example, I do not embrace the day Victoria died and prefer to focus on happier memories we shared together. The key is to not avoid or isolate on those days, thus empowering a painful memory. You have the power to mitigate painful memories by engaging in happy, tranquil, or friend-filled activities, particularly on those dates. You'll be glad you did.

Step 2: Fully Engage Companionship

Second, as you wade into Thrive, I encourage you to fully engage companionship. I'm not necessarily talking about new romantic relationships here (although that is certainly a possibility). Rather, I'm talking about companionship in the broader sense. Join clubs, do things with groups, become active in a local faith community, stay involved in sports and activities that you've always enjoyed, and maybe even pick up a new team sport or class with other people. In general, I'm saying you should strive to be part of the community. Get out in the world! You have so much to offer, and it would be a tragedy if you allowed your loss to isolate you from society. Your healing journey likely kept you in hiding for a while as you took care of your heart and soul, but by Thrive, that healing journey should be leading you back out into the world.

Step **3**: Take Care of Your Body

Third, as we've said before, make sure you are taking care of your physical health. This means getting plenty of rest, plenty of exercise, and plenty of *good* food. Note the word *good* there! My wife has a PhD in Preventative Health, and she spends a good portion of every day talking to people who have allowed their physical health to fall off a cliff. Many of them did so after a painful loss, as they simply stopped caring about themselves for a while. However, that only compounded their problem, because now they have frightening physical ailments on top of their seemingly overwhelming emotional pain. It's a double whammy, and it's one that can easily be avoided. By taking care of yourself and investing in the one body you have, you will be able to have the health, energy, and ability to continue thriving even if you are confronted with future heartache and loss.

Step **4**: Share Your Story, Wisdom, and Experience

Fourth, you can take Thrive to the next level by sharing your story, wisdom, and experience with others going through the early days of a similar loss. There are plenty of people who need to discover what you've just learned, who need the hope of knowing healing is possible in the face of tragedy. You have that hope. You worked for it, you fought for it, and now it's yours to share with others—just as others (hopefully) shared it with you along your journey.

In the world of twelve-step recovery programs, participants are encouraged to become sponsors surprisingly early in the process. A sponsor in that context is not an expert, teacher, or counselor. In fact, the only requirement is that the sponsor is himself a fellow addict who is working the twelve steps. The reason addicts are led to sponsor others so quickly is not just so they can help someone else; it's because the act of helping *others* ensures the sponsor will take *his own* recovery more seriously. That's what I encourage you to do: keep your own healing front and center by sharing it openly and honestly with other people. In doing so, you're not only bringing blessing and encouragement to them, but you're also making yourself publicly accountable to others. If they later see you slipping into an expected depression, they'll be there to hold you up. In this way, you become an even greater part of the companionship community we've discussed.

If you haven't started sharing your story and connecting with a community yet, our online community is a great place to start. We're an active group of people at every stage of the Survive-Alive-Thrive journey, and we would love to hear your story.

Step ⑤: Pursue Joy

While our faith response in Thrive (as well as Survive and Alive) should be characterized by prayer, Bible study, and forgiveness, I believe the most important spiritual step to take during Thrive is the act of pursuing joy. At this point, maybe for the first time since you began this journey, joy is not only a possibility but a likelihood. This is where you start to really believe that you can experience pure joy, fulfillment, and peace again. And, as a person of faith, I believe the very best expression of that joy is found in looking to God for the meaning in our journey.

If you're not at a place where you can accept this perspective, I only ask that you not write me off just yet. I'll talk much more about God's role in helping us experience true joy in section 3.

The Pursuit of Joy!

The Thrive season is to be embraced and nurtured. It's the point where you can enjoy the fruit of your labors, but it's by no means the end of the road. Rather, it's the beginning of a whole new chapter in your life story that still needs to be cultivated—lest the fruit you've grown starts to spoil. This life doesn't come with a pot of gold at the end of a rainbow. There's no big payoff this side of heaven. Life itself is the gift, and it's a gift that keeps giving all the way to the very end.

What's interesting as we've traveled the Survive-Alive-Thrive journey from loss to hope to happiness, is that we discover that there is actually another step! In fact, the term *happiness* has become so overused in American culture that it's meaning has been watered down to a temporal, fleeting definition for many of us. If we have a job, are paying our bills, are in a good relationship, and things are going well in a worldly sense, we are "happy." But when things go sideways, we suffer a loss, or we are struggling, we are no longer "happy."

Is that enough? How do we understand a poor farmhand working in the field of a Third World or economically impoverished country and singing joyfully in the process? What's up with Mother Teresa's seeming peace and fulfillment when she lived serving others in the streets of Calcutta? By American logic, she wasn't making Wall Street money or driving a fancy car, so how could she be "happy"?

So where do we go from here? In the next section, "Greater Than That," we're going to take the ultimate step and explore the quest beyond happiness—the pursuit of joy.

Questions for Discussion

1. What has been your biggest *healthy* emotional response as you've entered into Thrive?

2. Have you discovered a new sense of purpose as part of your healing journey? Explain.

3. This chapter talks about how our losses help us develop "thick skin" to better face future losses. How has your loss prepared you to face losses in the future?

4. What insecurities do you have about your new life?

5. How have you learned to deal with the loneliness that is so often associated with significant losses?

6. Some people use coping mechanisms such as food, alcohol, and relationships in unhealthy ways. How have you struggled with "too much of a good thing" and how can you guard against this?

7. What action step has been most helpful for you in entering into Thrive?

8. What does it mean for you to care for your own mental and emotional health? How can you best do that?

GREATER
—
THAN
—
THAT

Chapter 12

IN PURSUIT OF JOY

*T*HERE'S NO WAY TO SUGARCOAT IT: LIFE IS FREAKIN' HARD. IT punches you in the face, waits for you to get up, and then punches you again. That is the nature of life. In fact, I wrote this book through the spring and summer of 2020, a year marked by an unprecedented global pandemic. That was a *hard* year for many, many people around the world. Not only have hundreds of thousands lost their lives to COVID-19, devastating their loved ones and families, but exponentially more lost their incomes, jobs, health insurance, and any sense of normalcy or security. In short, many people lost their hope.

As I watched the news, I saw people living in fear, "hunkered in a bunker," waiting for the storm to pass. However, those of us who have been through terrible loss know a secret: even when the storm passes, another will roll in sooner or later. Again, that's the nature of life: it punches us in the face ... *repeatedly*. As Sylvester Stallone's character Rocky says in *Rocky IV,* "The world ain't all sunshine and rainbows. You, me, nobody is going to hit as hard as life. But it ain't about how hard you hit, it's about how hard you can get hit and keep moving forward."[8] If you're reading this book, you already know that, because you or someone you love has just been knocked down by loss and you're on your knees searching for answers and support. The life you have known, the relationships and balance that once brought you such comfort, have been shaken, and now you're struggling.

Nothing will test and challenge your worldview like loss. Our losses stay with us. They're woven into the very fabric of our lives. They affect our physical, mental, and emotional health. They change how we see the world. They impact our relationships. They prepare us for the hits that haven't come yet. The wound of a loss will heal, but the scar remains. The good news, though, is that there's also an influx of blessings—gifts of grace we never saw coming that God rains down on us. All these things swirl through our hearts and minds as we progress through Survive, Alive, and Thrive. And, as we move forward into the new life ahead, we're forever changed by the loss, healing, *and blessings* we've experienced. We emerge a little (or a lot) different than we were before.

As we near the end of this book, I want to ask an important question—perhaps the single most important question we've addressed so far: Once we enter Thrive, how do we *stay* there and not let the losses we haven't faced yet swallow us up again? How do we live in the blessings without falling back into the spiral of pain the next time life smacks us around?

I believe the answer is to pursue a life of joy.

No, I'm not saying "choose joy," as I've seen on many bumper stickers. There's a big difference between *choosing joy* and *having joy*. I don't think joy is a choice; I think it's a gift. Moreover, I don't think loss disqualifies us from a life of joy. Rather, I think loss is a *prerequisite* for joy.

8   "Rocky Speech: It is about how hard you can get hit and keep moving forward." YouTube, July 6, 2010, https://www.youtube.com/watch?v=_J0Ahh3UxbM

What Is Joy?

First of all, I don't think we can talk about *blessings* and *joy* in this section without talking about God. Here's why: I believe both are firmly rooted in God. That is, there are no blessings and there is no joy *apart* from God. Even the Oxford English Dictionary makes this clear, defining *blessing* as "God's favor and protection." I'd take that a step further and say a blessing is God's presence and purpose *practically and tactically* intersecting in our life journey. That's a lot different than how we usually understand *blessing* in our American vernacular. We're more inclined to define it as *luck* or *good fortune* than as a gift of grace from a God who knows and loves us. But I'm not talking about getting lucky by finding a great parking spot; I'm talking about experiencing hope when all seems dark and you may feel lost. It may be a clear and stunning moment that amazes you, or it may come as a subtle insight or perspective that leads to relief from the heartache you're working through. It's the difference between focusing on thoughts that are related to your loss and an event or moment that literally gives us the strength to fight through our pain for another day. Those are the blessings God rains down on us.

So the fact is that the term blessing is actually *defined* as an event or experience with which God is involved or has the capacity to be involved in your life in any and all circumstances. Does that mean you have to believe in God to experience blessings? No. As the saying goes, "God believes in you even if you don't believe in Him." He's still there working in the world and even working in your life. He still loves you and wants good things for you, even if you can't (or won't) see Him. If God truly is *greater than that*, then He's greater than your doubt and disbelief. He can send blessings your way with or without your attention. So if a *blessing* is God intersecting our lives, what is *joy*?

Joy Is Shaped by Your Faith/Worldview

Let's start with how we're wired. We've said throughout this book that our reaction to loss is largely impacted by our worldview, and our worldview is tightly tied to our backstory. That means those of us who grew up in Christian homes or with a generally faith-centered worldview will likely take to this faith-focused insight and encouragement much easier than someone who didn't. While loss is painful for everyone regardless of our backstories, most of us struggle to understand how and why something like this could happen to us. This is the moment when our worldview is proven under pressure. It can either yield a priceless diamond ... or it can crumble into dust.

If we believe our value is driven by our social status, how much money we make, the car we drive, or the size of our home, we won't survive under the pressure. The status symbols we cling to will come crashing down around us as we're thrust into the pain of questioning everything we thought had meaning. On the other hand, if you see the world through the lens of a life-giving hope that's greater than yourself, you're more likely to find healing and even joy in your journey.

For example, when you're dealing with the grief associated with the death of a spouse, nothing else seems to matter, particularly in the early stages of the loss. Such brokenness can be unbearable, and your mind races to process your pain through the filter of the worldview you've developed since childhood. If your worldview is defined by your status, you might be terrified trying to figure out how to maintain your standard of living without your late spouse's income. If your worldview is defined by your relationships, you might question who you are without your spouse. If your worldview has been shaped by a particular faith that promised a happy, pain-free life in exchange for your obedience to a particular set of rules or theology, you might question the existence of God for the first time in your life. After all, if you're taught that God won't let bad things happen to good people, you have no choice but to ask, *Am I not a good person?* or, *Did God lie?* or even, *Is God really there, or is everything I've been taught to believe a lie?* In these examples, you're not only struggling with the loss of a spouse; you're struggling with a complete breakdown of your entire worldview. That can make the concept of pursuing joy seem like a far-off wish—if not downright impossible.

Depending on your worldview, you may blame God for not intervening or assume He's not really there at all. If that's where you are, I challenge you to push back on the precepts you've held throughout your life and bear with me as I suggest an alternative.

Joy Is Inherent to a Faith-Centered Worldview

As I worked through my wife's death and the other key losses in my life, I was greatly comforted by the knowledge that I was not alone. You may have noticed that's a phrase I've said several times throughout this book: *You are not alone.* I have done this with intent, because I know from working with grief-stricken people how alone they can feel. That's why I encourage people to participate in communities and grief groups when they're working through a loss, because connecting with other people gets right to the heart of healing. Connecting with God, though, gets right to the heart of joy.

So our question, then, is: What is joy? I would argue that joy is the peaceful awareness of God's presence in our lives in both good times and bad. Kay Warren takes this a step further, arguing that, "Joy is the settled assurance that God is in control of all the details of my life, the quiet confidence that ultimately everything is going to be alright, and the determined choice to praise God in every situation."[9]

That may sound impossible to achieve if you're sitting at ground zero—day one of your journey through loss. I'd agree with you—*if* we see joy as something we have to *do* or *choose*. But that's not what joy is.

9   Kay Warren, *Choose Joy: Because Happiness Isn't Enough* (Revell, 2013).

Joy is a gift, something we *receive,* not something we have to *earn.* I love the promise of Psalm 16:11: "You make known to me the path of life; you will fill me with joy in your presence, with eternal pleasures at your right hand." Likewise, Galatians 5:22–23 lists joy as one of the fruits of the spirit, a natural outgrowth of a life of faith. Again, it's something we *receive* not *achieve.*

However, depending on your view of God, the thought of His persistent presence may not be all that reassuring. Some view Him as a master puppeteer—an uncaring, unfeeling deity who created the universe and then checked out, only returning to pull our strings for fun. That sounds like an all-powerful jerk to me. Others view Him as an angry, Bible-thumping, rule-loving judge, jury, and executioner who's just waiting to strike us down the second we do, say, or think something that breaks one of his precious commands. The idea is that all you have to do is work and work and work and work your entire life, never making a mistake and never taking a wrong turn, and God will lead you to the pot of gold at the end of the rainbow. This view of God seems especially hopeless to me. I don't know about you but I've screwed up *a lot.* And I'm going to screw up even more in the future. I can't place my trust in a God who's waiting to pounce whenever I make a mistake. More importantly, I wouldn't want to be around a person— or a deity—like that. I can't imagine trying to walk on eternal eggshells every second of the day.

On the other hand, if your pursuit of joy is found in a loving, involved, personal, grace-filled God who knows you personally, who feels your loss, whose heart aches with yours, who has experienced the pain of losing His beloved, and who is there to walk with you as a friend on this journey, you can have an entirely different experience.

Through Jesus, God shows us that we are indeed lost, sinful, and broken ... but He loves us anyway. He loves us so much that He wanted to come live among us and experience all the highs and lows of human life here on earth to provide a way for us to then join Him in heaven for all eternity. He made a way for us, in our imperfection, to engage a perfect God in a personal relationship. In doing so, He not only became our Savior, He became our friend—a friend who literally moved heaven and earth to stand with us, walk with us, and, when necessary, to carry us through our brokenness.

Will it make the pain hurt less? No, at least not in my experience. My God never promised me a life free of loss; rather, the God I know has experienced pain and loss Himself through the tortuous death of His Son. He knows where I've been, where I'm going, and most importantly, what I'm going through right now. In that truth, I can trust Him on the journey no matter how dark or difficult it may be.

I felt His presence and support every moment in the days after Victoria's death. He experienced it with me, not as a God who was too far removed to experience pain, but as a God who knew my pain all too well. I can't tell you what a difference that made to me, and I've never been more thankful for a worldview that acknowledged both the existence of a loving God and the reality of suffering.

What's the Big Deal about Jesus?

I've found that many people are perfectly comfortable talking about God, but the minute the conversation moves into Jesus territory, they can shut down. There's something about the name of Jesus that takes a conversation about God out of the clouds and brings it down into the nitty-gritty reality of life on earth. Many people aren't ready for that. If that's you, then buckle up, because I am compelled to talk about Jesus for a couple of pages.

In the face of loneliness and isolation in times of loss, joy is the acknowledgment that we are not, nor have we ever been, alone. God is with us. That's the very promise of the Christmas story: In Matthew's Gospel, an angel appears to an understandably hesitant Joseph and reassures him of the prophet Isaiah's words, " 'The virgin will conceive and give birth to a son, and they will call him Immanuel' (*which means*

'God with us')," (Matthew 1:23, emphasis added). So one of Jesus's names literally means God with us. Then, when Jesus was born, an angel appeared to some nearby shepherds. The first words out of the angel's mouth were, "Do not be afraid. I bring you good news that will cause great *joy* for all the people" (Luke 2:10, emphasis added). A while later, a group of Magi, or wise men, followed a star to Jesus. When they found Him, the Bible says, "they were *overjoyed*" (Matthew 2:10, emphasis added). Over and over throughout the Bible—and more directly, over and over through my and others' experiences—joy is found in the presence of God.

Joy is found in God's presence, and the door to that relationship is Jesus. Jesus is how we know and approach God. Jesus didn't come to start a new religion or create Christians—despite popular (and unpopular) opinion. Rather, Jesus articulated His role quite clearly. Yes, He claimed to bring a way of life that led to eternal life through Him, but He was also concerned with life here on earth. He sought to bring comfort, hope, and peace to those struggling with the most tortuous circumstances imaginable. In John's Gospel, Jesus says, "My purpose is to give [people] a rich and satisfying life" (John 10:10 NLT). Who was He talking about here? He was talking about His friends, neighbors, and followers. He was talking about the sick, scared, and hurting. And—get this—He was talking about the hated, marginalized, and outcast. Jesus was eager to share His message with the most righteous Jew and the most reviled sinner. He didn't care. He didn't come to build a small, selective church of brainwashed do-gooders; He came to make life better for everyone. He offers a great, big, wide-open tent and calls us all to join Him inside.

Jesus broke all social and religious barriers by talking to a prostitute in public (Matthew 26:6–7). He boldly disregarded racial stigmas and discrimination by addressing a Samaritan—a despised race among the Jewish people—at the community water well (John 4:1–26). He dined with tax collectors, who were considered traitors by their own people (Luke 19:1–9). When He was called out by the "proper" religious people of the time, Jesus pushed back on them *hard*. In Matthew's Gospel, a group of priests challenge Him for his big-tent message, and Jesus snaps back, "I tell you the truth, corrupt tax collectors and prostitutes will get into the Kingdom of God before you do" (Matthew 21:31 NLT). Does this sound like a churchy, overly religious, stuck up, rule-following Bible-thumper to you?

God as a Companion and Friend

Yes, I'm a follower of Jesus Christ, but I'm not interested in getting into apologetics here. All I want to do is suggest that a relationship with God is possible and can bring immense comfort in your time of loss. And I personally believe that Jesus is the only way to truly know God and draw near to Him. I'm *not* talking about a religion; I'm talking about a *relationship*, and a relationship with Jesus transcends corporate religion. In John's Gospel, Jesus tells His closest followers:

> My command is this: Love each other as I have loved you. Greater love has no one than this: to lay down one's life for one's *friends. You are my friends* if you do what I command. I no longer call you servants, because a servant does not know his master's business. Instead, *I have called you friends*, for everything that I learned from my Father I have made known to you. (John 15:12–15, emphasis added)

Jesus came to earth to do and be what He claimed and taught. From the start of my faith journey, he was my *friend*. A far-off, distant God is no help in times of loss. Neither is a set of rules that paints a perfect picture no one could live up to. But a friend? A friend is exactly what you need when your heart is broken into a million tiny pieces. And a loving God with the heart of a friend is the only one who can help you put those pieces back together into a new life scarred by pain but blessed with joy.

A Leap of Faith

I started my faith journey by acknowledging a hole in my heart that I couldn't fill. I discussed this in detail in the first chapter of this book. Nothing I did gave me a sense of completion or satisfaction—and I tried a lot of things. Money, career, relationships, social standing . . . it all fell far short. I've since come to believe that's how we're built. I think God designed us with a missing piece that only He could fill so that we would always be hungry for a relationship with Him, no matter how good (or bad) our lives are at any given time.

That missing piece led me on a historical examination of the facts surrounding Jesus. I tend to wrestle intellectual debates to the ground, so I dove into this issue head-first when my brother challenged me to defend my anti-God views decades ago. I figured it'd be easy to refute his faith-filled arguments with cold, hard, scientific facts and historical arguments against Jesus's life on earth. Boy, was I wrong. The more I read, the more I realized the preponderance of evidence actually falls on the side of Jesus—by a landslide. To my surprise, I came to learn that the Bible itself is just as historically valid—if not more so—than most of the ancient texts we accept without question. Books such as C.S. Lewis's *Mere Christianity* stunned me with the veracity and thoughtfulness of the intellectual debate, and more recent works such as Lee Strobel's *The Case for Christ* bring a skeptic's worldview face-to-face with the historical evidence of Jesus's life.

The result of this conflict between skepticism and historical reality was, for me, a leap of faith. Hebrews 11:1 describes faith as "confidence in what we hope for and assurance about *what we do not see*" (Hebrews 11:1, emphasis added). Likewise, Jesus told his disciple Thomas, who originally didn't believe reports of Jesus's resurrection, "Because you have seen me, you have believed; blessed are those who *have not seen* and yet have believed" (John 20:29, emphasis added). Faith is *not* blind trust. It is risking belief in something based on the evidence presented to our minds *and* our hearts. I had seen enough historical and factual evidence to get me 90 percent the way there. The last step—or *leap*—required faith.

If that's where you are right now, believe me when I say I understand. I'm not trying to force you into a decision either way. All I can do is faithfully represent the experience I've had and the experiences that hundreds of others have related to me. For us, those experiences point irrefutably to the fact that our joy on this side of loss is 100 percent due to God's presence in our lives. If you aren't there yet, don't worry. I'm no more interested in beating you over the head with a religious stick than I would have been if my friend Steve had done that to me at the start of my walk with Jesus twenty years ago. I am much more excited to explore the more *practical* realities of pursuing a life filled with joy.

As such, in the next chapter we'll complete the journey by exploring why joy is so important to us as survivors of loss and why and if we even need it in our lives.

Questions for Discussion

1. What does *joy* mean to you?
2. Respond to the statement, "Our losses are woven into the very fabric of our lives." How do we see this truth play out?
3. What's the difference between *choosing* joy and *pursuing* joy?
4. How has your worldview driven your understanding and experience of joy?
5. Name some practical benefits you have gained or would like to gain by pursuing a life of joy.
6. How do you respond to the idea that joy is a gift from God rather than something we can earn/achieve on our own? Is that good news or bad news to you?

Chapter 13

WHY *JOY?* ISN'T *HAPPINESS* ENOUGH?

——

At this point, you may be wondering, *What's the big deal about joy, anyway? Isn't it basically the same as happiness? Can't I just be happy about being happy?*

The Limits of Happiness

If you have been through a significant loss and you consider yourself to be happy again, then that is absolutely something to celebrate. There were days early in Survive when I thought I'd never feel happy again. Sure, I got to where I could laugh and engage with other people. Ten days after Victoria's death, our family and friends gathered for a post-memorial luncheon where we told stories, shared memories, and laughed together. That whole day, as sad as it was, was a celebration of her life. I was determined to feel *some* happiness mixed in with all my sorrow. Looking back, I consider it a major victory in my healing journey that I was able to enjoy so much of that day.

So, yes, you can and should be happy about being happy. It is a huge accomplishment and milestone in your healing. My point here, though, is that there is more to life than happiness. Happiness is situational, temporal, and shallow. It is *situational* in that it is usually associated with a specific event or interaction. I can feel happy about my performance during a high-pressure sales meeting, or I can feel happy about how well my son did in a track competition. It's an emotional response to an event, not a continual state of being. It is something I *feel*, not something I *am*. As such, happiness is swayed by the events of the day.

Likewise, happiness is *temporal* because the *feeling* of happiness doesn't last forever. In fact, because it's situational, happy feelings may only last mere moments. For example, if your boss gave you a big raise at 3:30 p.m., you'd no doubt feel happy even if you'd been annoyed all morning. Then if you got a phone call at 3:35 p.m. from a paramedic telling you your husband had been in a terrible car accident, you'd immediately go from happy to panicked. If your husband personally called back at 3:40 p.m. to let you know he was okay, the sound of his voice would instantly bring relief. If you heard a loud explosion just before the call was abruptly disconnected, you'd feel terrified. Annoyed to happy to panicked to relieved to terrified—all in about ten minutes' time.

Because it's situational and temporal, the feeling of happiness is ultimately shallow. Happiness comes and goes. It doesn't take much to make us feel happy. The entire advertising industry is built around creating these feelings for a product or service. We see thousands of ad impressions every week: web banners, pop-up ads, subtle advertisements in our social media feeds, TV and radio commercials, product placement in movies, junk mail, billboards, logo-branded clothing, and on and on and on. We can't escape it because advertisers know how important it is to make us feel happy—and they know how easy it is to do it.

However, if there's one thing we know for sure about happiness, it's that the feeling of happiness won't last forever. We're all one phone call away from bad news—news that can send us straight into a Survive season. The reality is that we are all human, and humans have a 100 percent death rate. None of us are going to make it out of here alive. That means our lives will be filled with health scares, accidents, surgeries, and a million other reminders of our (and others') mortality. Life will indeed keep punching us in the face until we ultimately can't get up anymore.

Now, if you put all your hope in happiness, that sounds like terrible news. However, if you aim higher, if you strive for the *joy* that lies just beyond happiness, life can feel much, much different. Happiness is feeling glad when something good goes your way. But joy . . . joy is feeling safe, secure, protected, comforted, and content anytime under any circumstance. Moreover, it's knowing you'll feel the same way tomorrow, next week, and next year, no matter what punches life may throw.

The Expanse of Joy

Have you ever seen someone who seems happy even though he *shouldn't* be happy? I'm talking about a person who has *nothing* the world tells us brings happiness. No money, no flashy car, no high-power career, no big house, no ritzy vacation photos on their Instagram feed—*nothing*. And yet, every time you see him, you're overcome with the sheer happiness radiating off of him. How does that happen?

Here's the secret: what you're seeing isn't happiness at all. It's joy.

The classic example is Mother Teresa. She spent her entire life working with people in the most impoverished areas of the world, perpetually surrounded by sick and dying people. She was bombarded by suffering on all sides. And yet, I've never seen a picture of her where she didn't have a joyful glow about her (if not a full, big smile). She had absolutely nothing we're told brings us happiness, but she had joy in spades. Why? Because her joy was found in her relationship with

God and in the calling He had put on her life. That enabled her to face the most nightmarish conditions with a song in her heart. She famously declared, "Joy is prayer; joy is strength; joy is love; joy is a net of love by which you can catch souls." Notice she's not talking about happiness; she's talking about joy. And joy doesn't depend on temporal success or the luxuries of modern life.

I've often noticed this spirit of joy in people facing much less dramatic circumstances. In an interview with a woman who was struggling with breast cancer, I was compelled when she reflected on her upbringing in South America, "We were poor, but I never realized it at the time. We had fun. We had food and basic clothing. We (usually) had a roof over our head. We loved each other. I didn't realize I was missing anything else. What can I say? We were happy."

I just smiled and said, "No, you *felt* happy. What you *were* was joyful. And that's a thousand times better."

I think this is what the apostle Paul meant in Philippians 3:7–9: "But whatever were gains to me I now consider loss for the sake of Christ. What is more, I consider everything a loss because of the surpassing worth of knowing Christ Jesus my Lord, for whose sake I have lost all things." Here, Paul is literally saying, "Everything I thought would make me happy I now consider nothing compared to God. There is absolutely nothing in the world that even comes close to the joy I have in walking with Jesus." And this is a guy who had it all before his decision to follow Jesus. He was a well-respected religious leader and an up-and-comer in ancient society. He gave that up to become a criminal in the eyes of the government and a hero in the eyes of the church. He didn't care about either, though. His eyes were on God, and his joy was set forever on a fixed point that no one could move or destroy.

How does that kind of deep, abiding joy change our worldview? Paul continued, "Do not be anxious about anything, but in every situation, by prayer and petition, with thanksgiving, present your requests to God. And the peace of God, which transcends all understanding, will guard your hearts and your minds in Christ Jesus" (Philippians 4:6–7). I see two big lessons in this verse:

1. We should not be anxious about our troubles. It sounds impossible, right? I mean, how can you tell someone in the face of the greatest pain of her life not to be anxious? It doesn't make sense! Well, that's because ....

2. This doesn't make sense! God's peace is so big and grand that it "transcends all [our] understanding." That means we can't even wrap our heads around the peace, comfort, healing, and sheer joy He has to offer.

That said, I live in the real world, and I've been where you are right now. Pain is real, and it is so very, very difficult. Your pain can sit on your chest like a boulder, stealing your breath, keeping you trapped, and slowly crushing you to death. There will be days when you can't move, when making it from morning to night without dying (or at least going crazy) will seem like a miracle. If that's where you are right now, I do not want to seem like one of those annoying, unhelpful "happy Christians" who tells you not to worry because God will take care of you. He will, of course, but I know that can feel like trite words of comfort when you're sitting in the pile of rubble that was once your life.

What I can tell you from experience and from my many conversations with people about their pain is that peace and joy *will* come. I can't explain how, when, or why; as even Paul the Apostle wrote that it "transcends all understanding" (Philippians 4:7). But I can tell you *who* and *where* it comes from: God, your friend and heavenly Father. It's not something you can achieve on your own, and it's not the result of self-reflection and self-actualization. Those may be important tools in your healing process, but they can't deliver the indescribable joy that God has made available to you.

Benefits of a Life of Joy

When I started a men's ministry at my church in Connecticut many years ago, I began by printing a single question on a flyer and distributing it around town. The question was simply, "What difference does knowing Jesus make in my life?" I was blown away by the responses I got from asking what I thought was an obvious question. Apparently, the men in my community were interested in cutting through the spiritual talk and getting down to the nitty-gritty about the real difference Jesus could make in their day-to-day lives. Could they be better husbands and fathers? Better businessmen? Better leaders? Better friends? To put it bluntly, they wanted to know what knowing Jesus could do for them.

I think the same is true when we talk about potentially lofty topics such as joy. We might relegate joy to a list of high-and-mighty ideals that sound good but don't really change anything in "the real world." Nothing could be further from the truth!

Joy makes a *huge* difference in our lives, not only in the aftermath of a horrible loss, but also in the context of daily life and the struggles we experience in business, relationships, health, and more. Here's a brief list of benefits we experience in everyday life when God's joy is working in our lives:

1. Reduced and mitigated stress, which rob us of love and quality of life.
2. Less uptight about life and fewer daily headaches, allowing us to work harder and be more productive free of the burdens of worry.
3. Statistically less lengthy and more manageable struggles for medical patients who are *joyful* while undergoing treatment compared to those who are *anxious and discontent.*

There are many, many more practical examples listed on our website, but you get the idea, I'm sure! In addition, of course, there's what I consider to be the most transcendent benefit of pursuing a life of joy, which is an overall sense of gratitude. Humble gratitude for the blessings we've been given is, sadly, increasingly rare in today's world. I believe many people in this generation—and, to be fair, many people in *every* generation—of our country have lived such blessed lives that they can't even see the blessings anymore. They don't know they're blessed any more than a fish knows it is wet. As such, people miss out on the incredible sense of gratitude that comes with acknowledging just how blessed we really are.

One of my favorite Christmas movies is *It's a Wonderful Life*. I watch it every year, and each time I'm taken aback by how negative George is in the first part of the film. He hates his job. He feels stuck in a town that doesn't appreciate him. He feels like he's missed his big shot in life. He feels like he's living a second-rate life. He has no idea how important he is to his family, his friends, and the entire town. Simply put, he can't see his blessings. As a result, he goes through life in a dark, poor-me fog, listlessly wandering from one day to the next with no purpose, no gratitude . . . no joy. It's hard to watch.

How many people do we know who act like modern-day George Baileys? We see them everywhere, and, when we see them, we avoid them like the plague! No one wants to get trapped in a roving pity party. People with no gratitude for what they've been given have a way of sucking the life out of other people. They're emotional vampires, draining our energy and stealing our enjoyment in life.

But what happened when old Clarence showed George his blessings one by one? George had a complete change of character. It wasn't just a mental shift or an emotional shift, either. George's entire life—his mind, heart, *and body*—changed. He was full of energy and enthusiasm. He was excited to get back to work. Even with the threat of being hauled off to jail for his uncle's mistake and Mr. Potter's despicable acts, he was at least thrilled that the officers knew who he was. Gratitude changed George Bailey's life completely and irrevocably. It can do the same for you.

Gratitude changes how you wake up in the morning, how you walk into a room, how you engage in relationships, how you go about your work, and how you view the world. It gives you a whole new lens through which to view the world—a lens tuned to all the incredible blessings God has provided. Gratitude is how two people can live the exact same day and have completely different responses. It reminds you that *you*—not the events of the day—get to decide whether you're having a good or a bad day.

Is the child singing on an airplane beautiful or annoying? Is your job a blessing or a curse? Are you grateful for the income you have, or do you feel undervalued? Are you happy to come home to a home-cooked meal or do you complain about your spouse being a bad cook? Is the guy on the subway with green hair and tattoos expressing his creativity or is he just a weirdo? These are the decisions we make every day that reveal a mindset of gratitude or a mindset of dissatisfaction. And these decisions determine what kind of day we're having.

I'm reminded of an old friend named Jim. Every time I asked Jim how he was doing in the later years of his life, he'd just smile and say, "I'm blessed." That smile cut right through me, because I could tell how genuine it was. He *was* blessed. More importantly, *he knew it*. That gave Jim a prevailing spirit of joy that was on display for all the world to see. I'm sure many people who met Jim came away sneering, "Huh. What's *he* so happy about?" They might never know. It's part of the "peace that transcends all understanding" that awaits those who pursue a life of joy in Christ.

How Do We Find This Joy?

So how do we achieve this wonderful joy that can, as Psalm 30:11 says, turn our mourning into dancing? We can't.

What?!, you may be thinking. *What do you mean we can't achieve it? What's the point then?*

Listen carefully: We cannot *achieve* joy. It's not a prize we can win or a goal we can attain. Rather, joy is a *gift*. It is there for the asking. Jesus says:

Ask and it will be given to you; seek and you will find; knock and the door will be opened to you. For everyone who asks receives; the one who seeks finds; and to the one who knocks, the door will be opened.

Which of you, if your son asks for bread, will give him a stone? Or if he asks for a fish, will give him a snake? If you, then, though you are evil, know how to give good gifts to your children, how much more will your Father in heaven give good gifts to those who ask him! (Matthew 7:7–11)

If we don't have to earn joy, if we can get it at no cost, does that make it cheap? Not at all. Just the opposite, in fact. God paid the highest price imaginable to be able to give us this invaluable gift of joy. Joy isn't *free*; it's a *gift*. Someone had to pay the price. It just wasn't us.

So What Do We Do?

This doesn't mean we're entirely off the hook, however. There are still things we can do to strive toward a life of joy, to fully realize the gift that's been freely offered. That's why I called this chapter "In Pursuit of Joy." The key word there is *pursuit*. So, instead of asking how we can *achieve* joy, we need to ask ourselves how we can *pursue* joy. I have two suggestions and a challenge.

First, get help. As I've said many times throughout this book, do not try to do this alone. Joy is best experienced in the context of community, so get out there and find others who are pursuing joy on their own journeys. Connect with a local church, join a small group, or find a grief group. If you aren't comfortable wandering into a church, then send some emails or make some phone calls to start building personal relationships with pastors in your area. If you click with one, then try meeting for coffee occasionally. Don't worry about being indoctrinated into the church or anything; just start by making a new friend like I did with Steve long ago. You can also connect with me and others in our online community. There's nothing quite like hearing people talk about their loss *and* their joy in the same breath!

Second, be intentional by making a decision to pursue joy. This may sound trite, but it is the most powerful thing you can do. Negative change happens automatically, but positive change starts with a decision. For example, nobody becomes overweight, out of shape, deep in debt, and bad at relationships on purpose. It just happens over time, usually because of inattention and neglect. But what *caused* the problem won't *solve* the problem. If you want to lose weight, get fit, be professionally productive or have a loving and supportive marriage, you have to make the decision to change the bad practices that got you into trouble in the first place. If you want to find joy, you've got to chase after it. You'll never just stumble into it accidentally.

Third, challenge yourself to give the pursuit of joy a try. Just for one day, focus your attention on the blessings in your life no matter what you're going through or what happens throughout the day. I'm certainly not suggesting you "put on a happy face" and act like everything's okay. If you're reading this book, everything is definitely *not* okay. Choosing joy isn't about turning a blind eye to the pain in your life; it's about opening your eyes to the blessings alongside the pain. So pick a day and, from the moment your wake up to the moment you go to bed, try to force yourself to focus (and, when necessary, refocus) on the blessings in your life.

As you focus on your blessings, get out in the world and engage in your relationships. Don't lock yourself away from the world. Grieving and depressed people want to isolate; I know I sure did. But at least for this day, challenge yourself to get up, get dressed, and get out. Make plans with a friend, go to church, go out to eat . . . just do *something* with and around other people. Engaging in your relationships will bring you face to face with a whole world of blessings you may never have noticed but have never needed more.

Now, don't be frustrated when everything doesn't go your way and don't try to control-freak your way to joy. It won't happen. Things will go wrong. Problems will arise. You'll get some bad news. You'll get sick. Stuff happens.

Neither your pain nor your pursuit of joy will stop the world from throwing punches. When life jumps up and punches you, take the hit, acknowledge the pain, and then remind yourself of a blessing you're thankful for. You can feel pain and gratitude at the same time. We're adults, we're capable of complex emotions! The point is that you are not in control of every little detail of your life. In fact, you're in control of very few of the details of your life. That's okay. God's got you, He's with you, and *He* is in control. It takes a lot of pressure off us when we realize we're not the ones calling all the cosmic shots.

At the end of this day of focusing on blessings, take stock of how you feel. Make some notes about your experience, how your attitude was throughout the day, how people responded to you, how you reacted when life sucker-punched you, and so on. If you can, extend the experiment another day. If you need to take a day to recover, that's fine, but challenge yourself with another day of focusing on blessings soon. My prayer is that you'll notice a dramatic shift in your response to pain. No, it won't disappear, but it can become less hopeless. And in recovering from loss, hope is the fuel that keeps you moving forward.

Everything Is Going to Be All Right

As we wrap things up, I want to go back to Kay Warren's definition of joy: "Joy is the settled assurance that God is in control of all the details of my life, the quiet confidence that ultimately *everything is going to be alright*, and the determined choice to praise God in every situation." My guess is that, right now, you find it hard to believe that everything will ever really be all right. If so, take heart. As the apostle Peter exclaimed, "So be truly glad. There is wonderful joy ahead, even though you must endure many trials for a little while" (1 Peter 1:6 NLT). Or maybe you're reading this in Thrive and you think you've already "arrived" at joy. You might think your work is over and you can kick back and relax. Either way, I've got news for you: your journey isn't over yet.

The apostle Paul got word that one of the churches he planted had gotten a bit lazy. They figured Jesus would return any minute, so why work? Why try to better themselves? Why serve other people? They were just sitting and waiting for Jesus to show up and wipe all their troubles away. Paul wasn't having any of that. He wrote:

> And we urge you, brothers and sisters, warn those who are idle and disruptive, encourage the disheartened, help the weak, be patient with everyone. Make sure that nobody pays back wrong for wrong, but always strive to do what is good for each other and for everyone else. Rejoice always, pray continually, give thanks in all circumstances; for this is God's will for you in Christ Jesus (1 Thessalonians 5:14–18).

I find that exhortation fascinating. He encourages them to warn those who are idle, encourage and help those who are hurting, be patient with all the stupid things other people say, guard their emotional responses and outward reactions, and strive to do good regardless of their circumstances. That's a tall order. But what does he say immediately after this? What are the keys to this grace-filled way of life?

1. Step 1: Rejoice always.
2. Step 2: Talk to God.
3. Step 3: Strive to be grateful at all times, regardless of your circumstances.

It's almost like Paul is talking directly to us as we go through Survive, Alive, and Thrive.

So what can we do to prevent ourselves from becoming idle, isolated, ungrateful, and joyless? I think the answer is in Paul's admonishment to "strive to do what is good for each other and for everyone else." We'll talk about that in the next and final chapter as we bring this book to a close.

Questions for Discussion

1. What's the difference between joy and happiness?
2. Describe a time in your life when you considered yourself to be joyful. Do you think you can ever feel that way again? Why or why not?
3. Why do some people seem so happy when there's no outward reason for them to be? What could we learn from them?
4. Has someone's sense of joy or happiness ever irritated you? If so, why?
5. How might an "attitude of gratitude" change how you live each day?

Chapter 14

GIVING BACK

#GodandLoveAlwaysWinintheEnd

IN HIS DEVOTIONAL *UNTO THE HILLS*, THE GREAT BILLY GRAHAM declares, "The sufferer becomes the comforter in the service of the Lord."[10]

I have been the sufferer and at times it has been a tough road to travel. Along the journey, I've come to learn that all that suffering has come with a brilliant silver lining: it has equipped me to share the good news of God's grace and goodness, a word of hope to a dark and hurting world. You see, I haven't *only* been through brokenness; I've been through a miraculous restoration. God walked with me through the "valley of the shadow of death" (Psalm 23:4 ESV) and brought me out the other side to testify to His grace. Along the way, He allowed me to cross paths with other men and women on the same journey, which has been a source of inspiration

---

10 Billy Graham, *Unto the Hills: A Daily Devotional*, "November 10," (Nashville: Thomas Nelson, 2010).

and healing for me. I've seen God work in indescribable ways in my life and in the lives of others. The healing I've seen in even the darkest of circumstances is nothing short of supernatural. And yet, while we've seen many blessings in our suffering in this final section of the book, I believe the greatest blessing of all is the opportunity to find joy by helping others. As we bring this book to a close, let's take a quick look at what that might look like.

Blessed to Be a Blessing

While I can't guarantee all your problems are over or that you've already been through the worst pain of your life, I can promise you that you have already learned more about victory through loss than most people ever realize. Your life, your loss, your healing journey . . . they've given you unique training. You've been drafted into the special forces, and your experience has giving you a master class in navigating through loss, redis-covering hope, and reclaiming happiness and joy. Those are powerful tools—tools you can put to work to change the lives of hurting people all around you.

Throughout each of the Survive-Alive-Thrive stages, we discussed practical steps you can take to maximize your healing and shift your focus away from yourself and toward others who are going through heartache of their own. Do not ignore these tasks! They will change not only your life but also the lives of many others God may bring your way. Share your story. Get in the weeds with others in their loss. Deliver dinners to hurting families. Make yourself available. Sit knee-to-knee with other people in grief groups. Seek out organizations like the many others listed on our nonprofit website to discover new outlets for sharing and applying the lessons you've learned. There is a world of people out there who need your help, who need the benefit of your experience. Go find them!

Love, grace, and mercy. These are the most important things, according to a woman who spent two years with me in a grief group. When I interviewed her about the loss of her five-year-old son who died in a tragic car accident, she said:

> I just want people to learn how to love each other. At the moments where it's so easy to get angry at people and hold grudges . . . just love and remember that there's always going to be a time when you're broken. There's always going to be a time when your partner's broken. We all need each other. Love and grace and mercy. Just pass it around, and we'll all make it through one way or another. That's all it takes: love, grace, and mercy.

Walking Together

As we bring this book to a close, I want to thank you. Thank you for allowing me to walk this road with you. Thank you for trusting me to share a little insight that, hopefully, has enabled you to see your loss through a new lens and will help you carry on from this point. I know from experience that trust can be hard to come by when you're feeling scared and alone. But if there's one takeaway I want you to carry away from this book, it's that you are, in fact, *not* alone. You are one of us now, a member of the fraternity of the brokenhearted. You have been through a tough and challenging loss. Maybe you're still going through it. Perhaps you've been on the receiving end of a midnight call. Or maybe you've just reached the end of a loved one's long, hard road—only to discover *your* journey is just beginning. Or perhaps you are still trying to wrap your arms around a frightening circumstance such as a divorce, a diagnosis, a child's special needs, or the stress of becoming a parent's primary caregiver. Whatever the loss, wherever you are on your journey, you are not alone, as both God and the Survive-Alive-Thrive community are here with you.

Moreover, you will get through this. I know you may not see it now but trust me: you can and will rediscover not only happiness but joy if you keep taking the steps we've outlined in this book. Each difficult day will melt into the next. Each day will bring its own challenges, of course, but it will also bring its own opportunity for joy. There is love and laughter and lightheartedness ahead of you. There are days without fears and weeks without tears just on the horizon. It won't be an easy journey, but it is one you can conquer. I know this because I conquered it—and if I can, *you* can. I also know this because I've been blessed beyond measure to walk with hundreds of men and women who have been right where you are now. Some didn't think they had it in them. But they did. They kept moving. They kept growing. They kept healing. And today, they are thriving in ways they never thought possible.

Remember what we learned about personality and backstories. Don't run from who you are and don't ignore where you've come from. Lean into those aspects of yourself. Explore how and why these things cause you to act and react the way you do. And pay even closer attention to your worldview. Your attitudes about life and loss are largely shaped by how you view the world. If God hasn't been part of that worldview up to this point, I encourage you to give Him a chance. Test the waters as I once did. Read the Bible. Explore the history and philosophy of Scripture—even if you approach it as a skeptic like I did at first. Don't be afraid to ask God your questions, argue with Him about your loss, shake your fist to the heavens, or fall into His arms for comfort. He is there for all of it.

Last, as I've said several times throughout this book, be sure to seek connection with other people. Churches, grief groups, and online communities are all great ways to interact with other people going through loss. I especially encourage you to join me and my friends at www.SurviveAliveThrive.org. There, you'll be encouraged with additional resources, articles, and a community of fellow travelers. Plus, you'll be able to access many audio interviews with those who have walked a similar path to yours. The audio library includes the full interviews of all the people I've mentioned throughout this book, plus many, many more. Hearing their stories has been, without a doubt, the most personally meaningful part of writing this book. I know you'll be strengthened and encouraged by their stories just as much as I've been. And maybe you'll even be inspired to help others by sharing your own story. You have no idea who needs to hear from you and how important your story of loss and recovery can be to others.

You have come so far. You have been knocked down by the impact of your loss, struggled to get on your feet again, and worked hard at the healing process. The work you've done is not meant for you alone, though. You have a story to tell—one not of just loss, but of learning to live again. Open yourself up and share your journey from loss to hope to happiness with those around you. When you're ready, we'd love to help you help them.

A EULOGY FOR MY WIFE, VICTORIA

June 4, 2016

Greater Than That

Victoria was my wife. She was my friend, the mother to our son, Andersen, and the heart and "love-anchor" of our family. And she is gone. And I miss her terribly. And it has been hard and painful to lose her.

But God is greater than that.

As many of you know, Victoria suffered from depression that sometimes made life difficult for her. It started for her following a traumatic car accident in 2009 and was exacerbated when she was rear-ended a year later. My friends, depression is a serious and formidable disease. It is cunning, deceitful, and is often stigmatized in our society. It can make life miserable for those afflicted and is painful for those who love them.

But God is greater than that.

My wife took her life on Wednesday, May 25, 2016. She was a victim of the disease of depression. It is tragic, and we are all coping to understand it. But we will not allow the enemy to cause more pain by hiding behind his lies of guilt, shame, or embarrassment. If you suffer from depression, please take your disease seriously and be diligent with your medications. If you know someone who struggles with mental health issues, help them and take it seriously. I know it is hard.

But God is greater than that.

But I have good news for those of us gathered in her name today. For Victoria's life will not be defined or remembered by her death. She will be celebrated and remembered as a godly woman with a giving and gentle spirit. She was all about forgiveness and being forgiven. A woman with the fierce heart of a mother-warrior committed to seeing the son she loved succeed and triumph as an overcomer.

She is so incredibly proud of Andersen and the growth he has shown as he has matured to become an honorable, young, strong man with a kind and tender heart. She had the unique ability to fight for what she knew was in the best interest of those she loved but to do so with an overarching kindness. That is rare.

But God is greater than that.

Of course, I have had the gift of a more intimate and personal relationship with the woman I fell in love with twenty-nine years ago on a business trip to Hawaii. We were married over twenty years ago on a scuba diving trip in Cozumel, and we had a lot of great adventures together. The Victoria I know and will always remember was smart, determined, and successful. She had an insatiable appetite for information. She could be tough. She was strong. She was beautiful. And sexy. She made me want to be a better man. I loved her deeply. And now my angel-heart is gone. And it hurts.

But God is greater than that.

I have heard often these past ten days that "I loved Victoria so much." I get it. I did too. She was a lovable person. There is a saying that says, "Long after you meet someone, you do not necessarily remember what they said, but you will always remember how they made you feel."

Her memory will live on for those who met her as a woman who made you feel that she genuinely cared about you. And you know what? She *did* genuinely care about you.

For those struggling to understand her death that seems incongruous after a recent encounter with Victoria, I have been blessed to hear and share many stories since her death. The common theme is that Victoria was at her best when she was focused on the needs of others. Her life will always be celebrated and cherished for that reason. Giving of herself to others was how she felt fulfilled and that is consistent with her desire to live a Christ-minded life.

But God is greater than that.

So where do we go from here? Victoria's story is not over. Yes, her time with us has come to an end here in New Canaan, but not our time with her in a much more important context. For those who love Jesus Christ, there is no doubt that eternal life with Him is promised and assured.

The Bible and teaching we believe are clear that Victoria is now with our Father in heaven. But sometimes God is merciful and generous enough to make Himself crystal clear on this issue. I have been blessed these past few days to hear of a couple of events where God has revealed Victoria's presence since her death, and I'd like to share one now (as I have been given permission to do so by our friend Karen):

Karen lives in Tulsa, Oklahoma. She is a Christian sister and friend from Grace with whom we enjoyed Dinosaur BBQ with our mutual friends Toni and Marc after service many times. On Thursday following Victoria's death, Toni called Karen to inform her of the situation. Like many of us, Karen was heartbroken, and she was also troubled by the fact that Victoria had taken her own life. Despite biblical clarity and theological assurances that the form of death has no implication on your eternal destination, with Doug (her husband) out of town, she went to bed early with a burdened heart. At 2:00 a.m., Karen explains that she was awakened by the material and physical presence of the Holy Spirit, angels, and maybe Jesus Himself. She had a sensation of angels' wings fluttering close and surrounding her. It was so real, she slowly reached over to turn on the light on her bedside table as she thought this could be the time she would actually see Him face to face. But as she turned on the light, there was no one there she could see. And then, at this moment, an audible voice from the Holy Spirit spoke to her and said, "She is with Me." For the sake of clarity, the voice repeated the same words: "She is with Me."

God is Great.

I want to take this moment to reach out to you on this topic. This is not religious. This is not political. It's not about philosophy. It's a true story about a Jewish guy 2,000 years ago who gave of Himself so we could all know peace. This is about my life, your life, and eternal life. If you know Jesus, hold Him closer. If you have not looked in His direction, He is there waiting to be with you. Right now. As we speak. Please, talk to someone who knows Jesus, give me a call, watch a program. Read a book. Do it your way. Just ask what it means to have a friendship with Him. Victoria would want you to so she could see you again.

Victoria can't come to us, but we can go to her. I know where she is and look forward to that day because of the grace and mercy of God through His son Jesus.

God is great.

Finally, I'd like to leave you with a quote that I am fond of from Richard Bach that takes on a much deeper meaning when considered in the context of eternal life:

Don't be dismayed by good-byes.
A farewell is necessary before you can meet again.
And meeting again, after moments or lifetimes,
is certain for those who are friends.
Victoria, I will see you again.

Thank you all.

Thank you for your prayers on behalf of Victoria these past ten days. Your support has been incredibly helpful and appreciated. God Bless you.

ACKNOWLEDGMENTS

WRITING THIS BOOK HAS BEEN AN EXTREMELY REWARDING WORK of passion for me and was only possible because of the many people who have participated across so many roles. If the term "it takes a village" were ever appropriate, this would be the time for it!

First and foremost, I'd like to thank those of you who have selflessly and transparently shared your experiences of loss and brokenness with me in interviews and one-on-one discussions over the past years. Each of your stories has inspired and touched me, and your capacity for empathy and grace will continue to serve as inspiration for others who journey down similar paths. I am honored to have spent time with each and every one of you.

To my pastors Cliffe, Chuck, Nathan, and Jackie: Thank you from the bottom of my heart for showing up when I needed you the most and providing God's words and wisdom in times of great struggle. I remain grateful to each of you for your love and support.

Stuart: I deeply appreciate your friendship as we partnered to support those navigating loss at Grace. I remain grateful for the insights you provided and the fun and laughter we shared in the process.

For the original FOV regulars including Kayla, Steph, Chris, Betty, and Dale: We are more than friends; we are brothers and sisters bonded together in the crucible of loss and brokenness. It is my joy and privilege to count you as friends.

My brothers Big Rob, Crazy Rob, K-D, and Sid: It is a great blessing in my life to call you friends. The support, feedback, and encouragement you have each provided along this journey means the world to me. What a joy to know that we stand in one another's corners no matter what the world throws our way.

Jim: You have inspired me since we met twenty years ago; what an amazing ride it's been! Thank you for your encouragement, support, and friendship along the way. You are a man after God's own heart, and I am fortunate to count you as a brother in Christ.

Allen: Who knew an editorial collaboration would reveal kindred spirits and lead to a deep and meaningful friendship! We are not done, my friend. There's so much more to do together and it would be great fun to keep the party going. Thank you from the bottom of my heart as I could not have done this without you.

Jonathan: What a fortuitous blessing to run into you at the Gentlemen's Cup! Your guidance, knowledge, and patience have made this book possible. Thank you for your support and encouragement. I am lucky to have partnered with you and Forefront Books on this adventure.

John and Carolyn: Although it is all that I have been blessed to know, I can't help but wonder if it is unusual to have such deep love, respect, and friendship with a brother and sister. I will never forget the acts of support and kindness you provided in my darkest moments on this journey. As for this book, thank you for your encouragement, proofreading, and feedback. I am a lucky man to have such extraordinary siblings.

And finally, Melyn: My amazing wife, friend, and confidant. Your kindness, giving spirit, and patience blesses me every day. That God has brought us together to share this journey is a miracle for which I will always be grateful. Your insight and support, particularly as we've navigated difficult subject matter, is nothing short of amazing. The tears we've spilled and the laughter we've shared have made it meaningful and rewarding. This book and the joy I experience every day would not be possible without you. #GodandLoveAlwaysWinintheEnd!